■SCHOLASTIC

D1239681

GRADES
3-6

WEEK-BY-WEEK

Phonics & Word Study

ACTIVITIES FOR THE INTERMEDIATE GRADES

Wiley Blevins

New York • Toronto • London • Auckland • Sydney
Mexico City • New Delhi • Hong Kong • Buenos Aires

Teaching *Resources*

Cover design by Jason Robinson
Interior illustrations by Teresa Anderko
Interior design by Kelli Thompson

ISBN: 978-0-439-46589-2

Text copyright © 2011 by Wiley Blevins.
Illustration copyright © 2011 by Scholastic.
All rights reserved. Published by Scholastic Inc.
Printed in the U.S.A.
5 6 7 8 9 10   40   17 16 15 14

Contents

* Each week introduces a set of 10 of the top 322 syllables for fluency review work. The exceptions are cumulative review and assessment weeks (10, 20, and 30).

Introduction

How to Use This Book

Reading multisyllabic words can be challenging for many of our students.

Some students, even those who seem to effortlessly decode one-syllable words, struggle when faced with longer, harder words because they haven't fully mastered those basic spelling patterns. That is, these readers lack the speed and automaticity required with those patterns to apply them to longer, more complex words.

Other students struggle when analyzing and breaking down a longer word into recognizable chunks that would aid in decoding. For example, rather than decoding a word such as *uncomfortable* sound by sound, we need students to instantly recognize the larger chunks *un*, *comfort* (or *com* and *fort*) and *able* to more easily tackle the word. Dealing with three or four pieces of information (*un*, *com*, *fort*, *able*) is much easier than dealing with 11 or more (*u*, *n*, *c*, *o*, *m*, *f*, *or*, *t*, *a b*, *le*).

The good news is that we can systematically and efficiently transition students from reading one-syllable to multisyllabic words if we take advantage of what they already know and make explicit those connections. Also, by focusing on high-utility decoding skills, syllables, and syllable patterns, we can tailor our instruction so that it is fast, efficient, and effective. This book will give you lessons, activities, and tips to help make that possible. Enjoy!

Weekly Schedule: Pacing

Scheduling intermediate phonics instruction into your daily plan can be easy and seamless: The lessons in this book take only about 10–15 minutes per day, and many of the activities can be completed during independent work time or used as warm-ups to your regular literacy block instruction. Below is a suggested weekly schedule for using the lessons and activity sheets in *Week-by-Week Phonics & Word Study Activities for the Intermediate Grades*.

Weekly Schedule				
Day 1	**Day 2**	**Day 3**	**Day 4**	**Day 5**
Whole Group • Introduce the week's new skill using the Mini-lesson (Part 1 of the lesson) • Syllable Fluency Flash Cards **Small Group or Independent** • Distribute the Speed Drill	**Whole Group** • Distribute the Activity Sheet for the week's new skill (e.g., Crossword, Word Search, What's My Word?) • Syllable Fluency Flash Cards **Small Group or Independent** • Have partners assess each other using the Speed Drill	**Whole Group** • Introduce the High-Frequency Syllable Fluency Activity (Have students begin the Part 2 Find It and Define It activities.) • Syllable Fluency Flash Cards **Small Group or Independent** • Have partners assess each other using the Speed Drill	**Whole Group** • Check the students' High-Frequency Syllable Fluency Activity Sheets (e.g., words with syllables found) • Syllable Fluency Flash Cards **Small Group or Independent** • Have partners assess each other using the Speed Drill	**Whole Group** 1) Published games 2) BINGO with High-Frequency Syllable Fluency Cards 3) Record words found with week's skill and syllables on classroom word wall 4) Collect Speed Drill forms and Activity Sheets 5) Syllable Fluency Flash Cards

Background Information

What Is a Syllable?

A syllable is a unit of pronunciation. Each syllable contains only one vowel sound. Finding the vowels in a word is an important starting point for breaking it apart by syllables. However, each syllable may have more than one vowel letter. For example, the word *boat* contains one vowel sound, therefore one syllable. However, the vowel sound is represented by the letters *oa*—a vowel digraph. In addition, whether or not a group of letters forms a syllable depends on the letters around it. For example, the letters *par* form a syllable in the word *partial*, but not in the word *parade*.

Have students who struggle with understanding or recognizing spoken syllables, place a hand under their chin. Then have them say a word, such as *understand*. Point out that each chin drop represents a syllable.

How Can Teaching Syllables Help Students Decode Multisyllabic Words?

To decode multisyllabic words, students must be able to divide words into recognizable chunks. Some readers develop a sense of syllabication breaks independently through their exposures to print; others have great difficulty and need instruction. When confronted with multisyllabic words, some students' phonics skills break down because they can't readily identify syllable boundaries.

Students can use syllabication strategies to approximate a word's pronunciation. This approximation is generally close enough for the reader to recognize the word if it's in the student's speaking or listening vocabularies. This demonstrates how important it is to help students develop their speaking and listening vocabularies and to combine building their background knowledge with vocabulary instruction.

Decoding instruction and vocabulary instruction are not mutually exclusive. In fact, at this level they overlap in very significant ways. Therefore, in *Week-by-Week Phonics & Word Study Activities for the Intermediate Grades*, I will show you ways to intertwine phonics and vocabulary instruction in order to maximize learning.

Why Teach High-Utility Syllable Spelling Patterns?

Teaching students an endless string of syllabication rules isn't the most effective way to enable them to read multisyllabic words. Too many rules are difficult to remember and apply, and many rules have limited application. Therefore, I recommend focusing on the six most common syllable types, or patterns, in English (Moats, 1995). Teaching and reinforcing these syllable types while decoding longer, more complex words will provide students with effective decoding tools.

Six Basic Syllable Spelling Patterns in English

1. **closed syllables:** These syllables end in a consonant. The vowel sound is generally short. This is one of the most common syllable types. (examples: <u>rab</u> <u>bit</u>, <u>nap</u> <u>kin</u>)

2. **open syllables:** These syllables end in a vowel. The vowel sound is generally long. This is one of the most common syllable types. (examples: <u>ti</u> ger, <u>pi</u> lot)

3. **consonant + *le* syllables:** Usually when *le* appears at the end of a word and is preceded by a consonant, the consonant + *le* form the final syllable. (examples: ta <u>ble</u>, lit <u>tle</u>)

4. **vowel team syllables:** Many vowel sounds are spelled with vowel digraphs such as *ai*, *ay*, *ea*, *ee*, *oa*, *ow*, *oo*, *oi*, *oy*, *ou*, *ie*, and *ei*. The vowel digraph appears in the same syllable. This is important as many students, knowing that each syllable has only one vowel sound, will mistakenly think that each syllable has only one vowel letter. However, vowel teams act as a team and can never be separated across syllables. (examples: r<u>oa</u>d w<u>ay</u>, ex pl<u>ai</u>n)

5. *r*-**controlled vowel syllables:** When a vowel is followed by *r*, the letter *r* affects the vowel sound. The vowel and the *r*, acting as a team, must appear in the same syllable. (examples: t<u>ur</u> tle, h<u>ar</u> d<u>er</u>)

6. **final *e* (silent *e*, magic *e*) syllables:** The final *e* vowel spellings, such as *a_e*, *e_e*, *i_e*, *o_e*, and *u_e*, also act as team and must remain in the same syllable. This is the most difficult syllable spelling pattern for students to recognize and can be taught last. (examples: com <u>pete</u>, de <u>cide</u>)

What About High-Utility Syllables?

When I travel to elementary classrooms across the country, I notice the countless hours spent helping students master the alphabet (the ABCs and their associated sounds) as well as the various spellings for the 44 sounds in English (e.g., the letters *ou* stand for the long *o* sound). These high-utility sound-spellings aid students in becoming efficient decoders of one-syllable words. However, I rarely see any time spent on teaching and reviewing high-utility syllables—those building blocks for multisyllabic words. For some reason, we stop. Let's not!

On the following pages, you will find a list of the 322 most frequent syllables in the 5,000 most frequent English words (Sakiey, Fry, Goss, & Loigman, 1980). By focusing on these syllables, we can give our students a leg up in their decoding of longer, more complex words. Over time, students will begin to automatically recognize these common syllables in words and use that knowledge to aid in their decoding. Each week in *Week-by-Week Phonics & Word Study Activities for the Intermediate Grades*, I will focus instruction on approximately ten of these syllables so that all can be covered and mastered by the end of the school year.

322 Most Frequent Syllables in the 5,000 Most Frequent English Words

1. ing	13. y	25. u	37. or	49. man
2. er	14. ter	26. ti	38. tions	50. ap
3. a	15. ex	27. ri	39. ble	51. po
4. ly	16. al	28. be	40. der	52. sion
5. ed	17. de	29. per	41. ma	53. vi
6. i	18. com	30. to	42. na	54. el
7. es	19. o	31. pro	43. si	55. est
8. re	20. di	32. ac	44. un	56. la
9. tion	21. en	33. ad	45. at	57. lar
10. in	22. an	34. ar	46. dis	58. pa
11. e	23. ty	35. ers	47. ca	59. ture
12. con	24. ry	36. ment	48. cal	60. for

61. is	98. no	135. sen	172. tin	209. cap
62. mer	99. ple	136. side	173. tri	210. cial
63. per	100. cu	137. tal	174. tro	211. cir
64. ra	101. fac	138. tic	175. up	212. cor
65. so	102. fer	139. ties	176. va	213. coun
66. ta	103. gen	140. ward	177. ven	214. cus
67. as	104. ic	141. age	178. vis	215. dan
68. col	105. land	142. ba	179. am	216. dle
69. fi	106. light	143. but	180. bor	217. ef
70. ful	107. ob	144. cit	181. by	218. end
71. ger	108. of	145. cle	182. cat	219. ent
72. low	109. pos	146. co	183. cent	220. ered
73. ni	110. tain	147. cov	184. ev	221. fin
74. par	111. den	148. da	185. gan	222. form
75. son	112. ings	149. dif	186. gle	223. go
76. tle	113. mag	150. ence	187. head	224. har
77. day	114. ments	151. ern	188. high	225. ish
78. ny	115. set	152. eve	189. il	226. lands
79. pen	116. some	153. hap	190. lu	227. let
80. pre	117. sub	154. ies	191. me	228. long
81. tive	118. sur	155. ket	192. nor	229. mat
82. car	119. ters	156. lec	193. part	230. meas
83. ci	120. tu	157. main	194. por	231. mem
84. mo	121. af	158. mar	195. read	232. mul
85. on	122. au	159. mis	196. rep	233. ner
86. ous	123. cy	160. my	197. su	234. play
87. pi	124. fa	161. nal	198. tend	235. ples
88. se	125. im	162. ness	199. ther	236. ply
89. ten	126. li	163. ning	200. ton	237. port
90. tor	127. lo	164. n't	201. try	238. press
91. ver	128. men	165. nu	202. um	239. sat
92. ber	129. min	166. oc	203. uer	240. sec
93. can	130. mon	167. pres	204. way	241. ser
94. dy	131. op	168. sup	205. ate	242. south
95. et	132. out	169. te	206. bet	243. sun
96. it	133. rec	170. ted	207. bles	244. the
97. mu	134. ro	171. tem	208. bod	245. ting

246. tra	262. cen	278. its	294. one	310. sons
247. tures	263. char	279. jo	295. point	311. stand
248. val	264. come	280. lat	296. prac	312. sug
249. var	265. cul	281. lead	297. ral	313. tel
250. vid	266. ders	282. lect	298. rect	314. tom
251. wil	267. east	283. lent	299. ried	315. tors
252. win	268. fect	284. less	300. round	316. tract
253. won	269. fish	285. lin	301. row	317. tray
254. work	270. fix	286. mal	302. sa	318. us
255. act	271. gi	287. mi	303. sand	319. vel
256. ag	272. grand	288. mil	304. self	320. west
257. air	273. great	289. moth	305. sent	321. where
258. als	274. heav	290. near	306. ship	322. writ
259. bat	275. ho	291. nel	307. sim	
260. bi	276. hunt	292. net	308. sions	
261. cate	277. ion	293. new	309. sis	

Word Study: Prefixes

The term "word study" refers to learning everything about a word, including its spelling, meaning, pronunciation, historical origin, and relationship with other words. Understanding affixes, such as common prefixes and suffixes, and Greek and Latin roots and combining forms, can aid students in decoding a word and determining its meaning. Throughout *Week-by-Week Phonics & Word Study Activities for the Intermediate Grades*, I will be focusing on those high-utility prefixes, suffixes, and Greek and Latin roots that will most benefit students' decoding and vocabulary skills. The following pages provide background information related to each topic.

Prefix Guidelines:

1. A prefix is a group of letters that appears at the front of a word. A prefix affects the meaning of the root, or base, word to which it is attached. To determine whether or not a group of letters is a prefix, remove them from the word. If a known word remains, then you are correct. For example, remove the letters *un-* from the following words: *unhappy, untie, uncle, uninterested*. In which word are the letters *un* <u>not</u> a prefix? Yes, these letters are not a prefix in the word *uncle*.

2. Make students aware of the following warnings about prefixes:

- Most prefixes have more than one meaning. For example, the prefix *un-* can mean "not" as in *unhappy*, or "do the opposite of" as in *untie*. Teach the multiple meanings of the most common prefixes and use careful language during lessons, such as "the prefix *un* <u>sometimes</u> means *not*."

- Be careful of letter clusters that look like prefixes, but aren't. For example, when the letters *un* are removed from *uncle*, no recognizable root word is left. In addition, when the letters *in* are removed from *invented*, the word that remains has no relation to the whole word. The prefixes that cause the most difficulty are *re-*, *in-*, and *dis-*.
- Don't rely solely on word part clues. Context clues must be used as well to verify a word's meaning. For example, a student might think the word *unassuming* means "not assuming/not supposing" instead of its actual meaning, "modest." It is estimated that about 15–20% of the prefixed words students will encounter share this complexity. (White, Sowell, & Yanagihara, 1989)

3. Teach only those prefixes that have high utility. The chart that follows shows the most common prefixes based on a count of prefixed words appearing in *The American Heritage Word Frequency Book* (Carroll, Davies, and Richman, 1971). The prefix *un-* alone accounts for almost one-third of the total. The top three prefixes account for over half.

Rank	Prefix	%	Rank	Prefix	%
1.	un- (not, opposite of)	26	11.	pre- (before)	3
2.	re- (again)	14	12.	inter- (between, among)	3
3.	in-, im-, ir-, il- (not)	11	13.	fore- (before)	3
4.	dis- (not, opposite of)	7	14.	de- (opposite of)	2
5.	en-, em- (cause to)	4	15.	trans- (across)	2
6.	non- (not)	4	16.	super- (above)	1
7.	in-, im- (in or into)	4	17.	semi- (half)	1
8.	over- (too much)	3	18.	anti- (against)	1
9.	mis- (wrongly)	3	19.	mid- (middle)	1
10.	sub- (under)	3	20.	under- (too little)	1

All other prefixes (@ 100) accounted for only 3% of the words.

Word Study: Suffixes

Suffix Guidelines:

1. A suffix is a letter or group of letters that is added to the end of a root, or base, word. Common suffixes include *-s*, *-ed*, *-ing*, *-ly*, and *-tion*. A suffix changes the meaning of the root word. Students, therefore, need to have an understanding of the meaning of suffixes or how they affect the meaning of a root word. In addition, helping students to quickly attend to suffixes in words will help them visually remove the suffix to identify the base word. This will help them figure out the meaning of the whole word.

2. Adding a suffix sometimes changes the spelling of a base word. Students need to be directly taught those suffixes that cause spelling changes. The three most common spelling changes resulting from the addition of suffixes are:

- consonant doubling (*runner, running*): The consonant is doubled so that the first syllable will form a CVC pattern. Most CVC words contain a short vowel sound (closed syllable). Therefore, the second consonant acts as a diacritical mark—it ensures that the short vowel sound of the root word is maintained.

- change *y* to *i* (*flies, happiest, loneliness*): Words that end in *y* change the *y* to *i* before adding a suffix. This is done because the letter *y* at the beginning of a word or syllable acts as a consonant and stands for the /y/ sound. However, the letter *y* at the end of a word either stands for a vowel sound (*fly*) or is part of a vowel digraph (*play*). The change from *y* to *i* ensures that the vowel sound the *y* stands for in the word is maintained.

- delete the silent *e* (*making*): When a word ends in silent *e*, the letter is removed before adding the suffix (except *-s*). Most of the common suffixes begin with vowels and this vowel doubling would cause confusion; it would create a vowel digraph.

3. Teach only the most commonly used suffixes. The chart that follows shows the 20 most frequent suffixes appearing in words in the *Word Frequency Book* (Carroll, Davies, and Richman, 1971). The suffixes *-s*, *-es*, *-ed*, and *-ing* account for almost two-thirds of the words. The suffixes *-s* and *-es* are used to form the plurals of most nouns. The suffixes *-ed* and *-ing* are inflectional endings added to verbs to change their tense.

Rank	Suffix	%	Rank	Suffix	%
1.	-s, -es (plurals)	31	11.	-ity, -ty (state of)	1
2.	-ed (past-tense verbs)	20	12.	-ment (action or process)	1
3.	-ing (verb form/present participle)	14	13.	-ic (having characteristics of)	1
4.	-ly (characteristic of)	7	14.	-ous, -eous, -ious (possessing the qualities of)	1
5.	-er, -or (person connected with)	4	15.	-en (made of)	1
6.	-ion, -tion, -ation, -ition (act, process)	4	16.	-er (comparative)	1
7.	-ible, -able (can be done)	2	17.	-ive, -ative, -itive (adjective form of a noun)	1
8.	-al, -ial (having characteristics of)	1	18.	-ful (full of)	1
9.	-y (characterized by)	1	19.	-less (without)	1
10.	-ness (state of, condition of)	1	20.	-est (comparative)	1

All other suffixes (@ 160) accounted for only 7% of the words.

It is beneficial to teach students the part of speech formed by each suffix. Note the following:

- **Noun Suffixes:** *-age, -al, -ance, -ant, -ate, -ee, -ence, -ent, -er, -or, -ar, ese, -ess, -hood, -ice, -ism, -ist, -ment, -ness, -sion, -tain, -tion, -ure*
- **Suffixes That Form Adjectives:** *-able, -al, -er, -est, -ette, -let, -ful, -fully, ible, -ic, -ical, -ish, -ive, -less, -ous, -some, -worthy*
- **Suffixes That Form Adverbs:** *-ly, -wards, -ways, -wide, -wise*
- **Suffixes That Create a Verb Form:** *-ate, -ed, -en, -ing, -ise, -ize, -yze*

Word Study: Greek and Latin Roots

English words are derived from three primary origins—Anglo-Saxon, Romance (Latin), and Greek (Moats, 1999). About 60% of the words in English text are of Latin and Greek origin (Henry, 1997). Words with Greek roots are common in science and social studies textbooks (Bear, Invernizzi, Templeton, & Johnston, 1996; Henry, 1988). Words with Latin roots are common in technical, sophisticated texts found in literature and upper-elementary textbooks. Words with Anglo-Saxon roots are common in everyday speech; these words are found in primary-level texts. The list below contains some of the most common Greek and Latin roots.

Teaching common Greek and Latin roots in the intermediate grades and beyond will help students access a larger number of words. These roots will provide clues to determine word meanings and help students cognitively group related words. I suggest teaching Greek and Latin roots in categories, such as roots related to number (*uni, bi, tri*) or the body (*ped, audi, man*). This will help students more efficiently sort and group words in their memories. It isn't necessary or reasonable to teach the meanings of all the roots and their corresponding words. The value is in teaching students key words that they can use to analyze unfamiliar words and to focus on the most common high-utility roots.

Common Greek Roots

auto: automatic, autograph, autobiography, automobile, autocracy
bio: biology, biosphere, biography, biochemistry, biometrics, biophysics
graph: graphite, geography, graphic, photograph, phonograph
hydro: anhydrous, dehydration, hydrogen, hydrant, hydrostatic, hydrophobia, hydrotherapy, hydroplane
meter: speedometer, odometer, metronome, thermometer, chronometer, perimeter, hydrometer
ology: geology, theology, zoology, meteorology, phonology
photo: photography, photocopy, photosynthesis, phototropism, photostat, photogenic
scope: periscope, stethoscope, telescope, microscope, microscopic
tele: telephone, telepathy, telegraph, television
therm: thermos, thermodynamics, thermostat, thermophysics

Common Latin Roots

audi: auditory, audience, audit, auditorium, audible, inaudible, audition
dict: dictate, predict, dictator, edict, contradict, dictation, indict, prediction
ject: reject, inject, projection, interjection, eject, objection, dejection
port: transport, transportation, import, export, porter, portable, report, support
rupt: rupture, erupt, eruption, interrupt, interruption, disruption
scrib/script: scribe, describe, manuscript, inscription, transcript, description, prescription
spect: spectator, inspect, inspector, respect, spectacle, spectacular
struct: structure, construct, construction, instruct, destruction, reconstruction
tract: tractor, traction, attract, subtraction, extract, retract, attractive
vis: vision, visual, visit, supervisor, invisible, vista, visualize, visionary

Bibliography

Bear, D. R., Invernizzi, M., Templeton, S., & Johnston, F. (1996). *Words Their Way: Word Study for Phonics, Vocabulary, and Spelling Instruction*. Englewood Cliffs, NJ: Merrill/Prentice-Hall.

Biemiller, A. (2009). *Words Worth Teaching*. New York: McGraw-Hill.

Carroll, J. B., Davies, P., & Richman, B. (1971). *The American Heritage Word Frequency Book*. Boston: Houghton Mifflin.

Coxhead, A. (2000). *A New Academic Word List*. TESOL Quarterly, 34, 213–238.

Harris, A., & Jacobson, M. (1982). *Basic Reading Vocabularies*. New York: Macmillan.

Henry, M. (1988). "Beyond Phonics: Integrated Decoding and Spelling Instruction Based on Word Origin and Structure." *Annals of Dyslexia, 38*, 258–275.

Henry, M. K. (1997). "The Decoding/Spelling Continuum: Integrated Decoding and Spelling Instruction from Pre-School to Early Secondary School." *Dyslexia, 3*.

Moats, L. C. (1995). "The Missing Foundation in Teacher Education." *American Federation of Teachers* (Summer).

Moats. L. C. (1999). "Teaching Decoding." *American Educator*, Spring/Summer. In Reading all about it. California State Board of Education.

Sakiey, E., Fry, E., Goss, A., & Loigman, B. (1980). "A Syllable Frequency Count." *Visible Language, 14*(2), 133–150.

White, T. G., Sowell, J., & Yanagihara. (1989). "Teaching Elementary Students to Use Word-Part Clues." *The Reading Teacher*, January.

Reading Big Words: Getting Started

Welcome to Week 1 of *Week-by-Week Phonics & Word Study Activities for the Intermediate Grades*. During this week, you will introduce your students to the strategies and instructional routines that will be used throughout the year. These include introducing your students to the Decoding Big Words Strategy, the procedure for using Speed Drills, and the High-Frequency Syllable Fluency routine.

INTRODUCE DECODING BIG WORDS STRATEGY

1. Distribute copies of the Decoding Big Words Strategy on page 17. Post a copy on a classroom wall or bulletin board.

2. Tell students that this strategy is a simple five-step process for decoding an unfamiliar word. They will practice this strategy throughout their word study lessons this year and while they read.

3. Walk students through the Decoding Big Words Strategy, using the word *unlisted*. Write the word *unlisted* on the board, but do not pronounce it. Rather, say: "Let's look at the word *u-n-l-i-s-t-e-d* (spell it aloud) to see how we can break it apart into recognizable or manageable chunks. This will help us read the whole word."

STEP 1

Look for the word parts (prefixes) at the beginning of the word. Explain that many common word parts can be found at the beginning of a word, such as *un-*, *dis-*, *re-*, and *pre-*. These word parts are called prefixes. They are added to a base word and change the word's meaning. Circle the prefix *un-* in the word *unlisted* and pronounce it.

STEP 2

Look for the word parts (suffixes) at the end of the word. Explain that many common word

parts can be found at the ending of a word, such as *-ed*, *-ing*, *-ful*, and *-ment*. These word parts are called suffixes. They are added to a base word and often change the word's part of speech. Circle the suffix *-ed* in the word *unlisted* and pronounce it.

STEP 3

In the base word, look for familiar spelling patterns. Think about the six syllable spelling patterns you have learned. Tell students that what is left (what isn't circled) is the base word. They should use their decoding skills to sound out this part of the word. Underline the base word *list* and pronounce it. Explain to students that this year they will also learn six common syllable types that will help them sound out the base word if they don't already recognize it.

STEP 4

Sound out and blend together the word parts. Slowly decode the word: *un-list-ed*.

STEP 5

Say the word parts fast. Adjust your pronunciation as needed. Ask yourself: "Is it a real word? Does it make sense in the sentence?" Read the word *unlisted* at a natural pace. Adjust the pronunciation as needed. (*Note:* This will be necessary in many multisyllabic words as one or more of the syllables will be unaccented.) Tell students that if they were reading a passage, they would check to see if this word made sense in the sentence they were reading. You will model this as they read throughout the year.

4. Have students work with partners to complete page 17. They will use the Decoding Big Words Strategy to decode four new words and then explain how the strategy helped them.

INTRODUCE SPEED DRILL ROUTINE

1. Distribute copies of the Speed Drill on page 18.

2. Tell students that a speed drill is a timed reading of a small set of words with the phonics patterns, syllables, or Greek and Latin roots they are studying. Learning this set of words well will help them recognize other words with the same spelling patterns, syllables, or roots.

3. Teach students the routine below for using speed drills. Explain that they will work with the speed drill all week (maybe longer) until they develop fluency with the targeted skill.

STEP 1

Underline the spelling pattern, syllable, or root in each word on the drill. Guide students as they do this. I recommend you time this (2 minutes) to add a game-like element and emphasize the importance of recognizing these patterns quickly (thereby building automaticity/fluency).

STEP 2

Help students pronounce the words on the speed drill. Each speed drill contains 20 words, and each word is repeated five times. You need to review only the words in the first two rows as these represent all the words in the speed drill. Model for students how to use the target skill to read the word. For example, on the sample speed drill on page 18, use the base word and the suffix -er or -or to sound out the larger word. Some of the words on the speed drill will stretch students' vocabularies. Ask volunteers to provide a simple definition for each one. State the definition for any words that your students don't know.

STEP 3

Time students as they read the words on the speed drill for 1 minute. I recommend that you pair students for the repeated timings throughout the week. You will not have the time to assess all students. Place a small timer in a learning center or have students use the classroom clock (if it has a second hand) to time their partner reading the words. Students should start at the top and read the words across as quickly as possible. Partners will note when the 1 minute is finished. The partner is also responsible for noting any misread words. That student then counts the number of words read correctly in 1 minute and records it on the page beside "Timed Reading 1."

STEP 4

Students practice reading the words on their speed drills during independent time and for homework.

STEP 5

Students are reassessed by their partner later in the week (when they feel ready) and record their new (and hopefully improved) time beside "Timed Reading 2."

STEP 6

Check timed reading scores for all student speed drills at the end of the week. Those students who need more practice to develop fluency will continue to practice reading the words on their speed drill. You will do the final timed reading and record that score beside "Timed Reading 3."

Note to Teacher: For Speed Drills with longer words and smaller print, you may wish to enlarge and photocopy them on a bigger sheet of paper.

INTRODUCE HIGH-FREQUENCY SYLLABLE FLUENCY ROUTINE

Distribute copies of the High-Frequency Syllable Fluency Part 1 activity sheet on page 19. This page includes the ten most frequent syllables in English. Also distribute copies of the Part 2 activity sheet on page 159. Students will:

PART 1

Read It: underline the syllable in each word, then use the words in a sorting activity

PART 2

Find It: look for other words with these syllable patterns in their weekly readings

Define It: record the meanings of five (or more) unknown words that appear on the chart to build vocabulary

Some useful information about the High-Frequency Syllable Fluency pages:

1. Throughout the year, **students will be exposed to the 322 most common syllables in the 5,000 most frequent words in English.** Learning these syllables will help students recognize them in new words while reading.

2. Some of the syllables will have different pronunciations based on their position in a word. For example, a syllable in an unaccented syllable will be pronounced with a schwa sound. **An asterisk (*) is placed beside any word in which the syllable has an alternate pronunciation.** Review these with students as you review the words on the page.

3. **The words in each column get progressively more complex.** Therefore, the words in column 3 are the most complex. If you are working with younger students, you may choose to only use the words in the first two columns. However, stretching students' vocabularies by using all three columns will be beneficial.

4. Some of the words in the High-Frequency Syllable Fluency Charts are **boldfaced.** These are words taken from Averil Coxhead's list of **High-Incidence Academic Words.** These are words that students will encounter in a lot of texts, but may be unfamiliar with. It is critical to focus attention on the meanings of these words as well as their common syllables. The other words on the page were chosen from Andrew Biemiller's *Words Worth Teaching* lists and the Harris-Jacobson *Basic Reading Vocabularies* lists.

5. Once you introduce each set of syllables for the week, create a set of **Syllable Fluency Flash Cards.** Each day, flip through the cards quickly as students chorally read them. Each week, add the new set of cards to the growing flash card set. This fast, 2-minute warm-up drill will help students gain automaticity in reading these common syllables and further help them recognize these syllables while reading.

6. Record the syllables on a chart in the classroom or a word wall. As students find words with these syllables in their weekly readings, have them add the words to the chart or word wall. You might wish to provide a prize each week for the students who find the most words. This will help **create an interest in and excitement about words** and make students active observers of words and their important parts.

Name _____ Date _____

Decoding Big Words Strategy

Decoding Big Words

1. Look for the word parts (prefixes) at the beginning of the word.

2. Look for the word parts (suffixes) at the end of the word.

3. In the base word, look for familiar spelling patterns. Think about the six syllable spelling patterns you have learned.

4. Sound out and blend together the word parts.

5. Say the word parts fast. Adjust your pronunciation as needed. Ask yourself: "Is it a real word? Does it make sense in the sentence?"

Use the Decoding Big Words Strategy to decode the words below. With a partner, discuss the information in each step that helped you determine how to pronounce each word.

Word: uncovered
Which Steps Helped Me: _____

_____

_____

Word: rebuilding
Which Steps Helped Me: _____

_____

_____

Word: disobeyed
Which Steps Helped Me: _____

_____

_____

Word: hopelessness
Which Steps Helped Me: _____

_____

_____

Name _____ Date _____

What Is a Speed Drill?

1. Underline the syllable -er or -or in each word.
2. Pronounce each word with your teacher.
3. Practice reading the words on your own.
4. When you are ready, have a partner time you reading the words for one minute. Keep practicing to improve your speed.

banker	boxer	senator	builder	conductor	dreamer	farmer	gardener	collector	visitor
rapper	auditor	sculptor	flier	writer	governor	climber	inventor	investigator	survivor
senator	rapper	boxer	builder	sculptor	dreamer	investigator	farmer	climber	gardener
survivor	collector	governor	auditor	flier	collector	writer	inventor	visitor	senator
conductor	investigator	banker	dreamer	conductor	farmer	gardener	boxer	governor	sculptor
flier	governor	visitor	survivor	senator	auditor	climber	rapper	banker	conductor
boxer	collector	inventor	gardener	climber	collector	sculptor	visitor	writer	builder
investigator	conductor	farmer	climber	banker	inventor	builder	survivor	gardener	rapper
rapper	writer	flier	sculptor	survivor	dreamer	investigator	auditor	inventor	farmer
dreamer	senator	auditor	builder	governor	visitor	flier	banker	writer	boxer

	Words per Minute	Date	Partner
Timed Reading 1	_____	_____	_____
Timed Reading 2	_____	_____	_____
Timed Reading 3	_____	_____	_____

Name _____ Date _____

High-Frequency Syllable Fluency • Part 1

Recognizing the Most Common Syllables in English

 Read It

1. Underline the target syllable in each word.
2. Practice reading the words.
3. Cut apart the word cards.
4. See how fast you can sort the words by common syllable.

Syllables 1–10

ing	pick<u>ing</u>	writing	**forthcoming**
er	never	**recover**	**practitioner**
a	alive	**abandon**	**adapt**
ly	silly	gladly	happily
ed	acted	decided	stranded
i	idea	iron	radio*
es	boxes	beaches	touches
re	recycle	**reinforce**	receptionist
tion	nation	motionless	relationship
in	inside	**individual**	reinstate

● For Part 2, make a copy of the reproducible on page 159 for each student.

Closed Syllables Mini-lesson

 STEP 1

Define

Tell students that a **closed syllable** ends in a consonant. The vowel sound is generally short. For example, each syllable in the word *napkin* (*nap* and *kin*) ends in a consonant and has a short vowel sound.

 STEP 2

Transition to Longer Words

Help students transition from reading one-syllable to multisyllabic words. Have them read the simple word in the first column, then use that word to read the multisyllabic word in the second column.

nap	napkin
cab	cabin
but	button
cut	cutlet
ten	tennis
kit	kitchen
den	dentistry
pan	panicky
pig	pigment
ran	randomly

 STEP 3

Build Words

Write the following word parts on the board:

tic, et, ic, fran, plas, tent, test, text, bask, jack, com, con, pan, rus

Have student pairs combine the word parts to build as many words as possible. These and other words can be formed:

frantic, plastic, content, contest, context, basket, comet, jacket, panic, rustic, comic

 STEP 4

Apply Decoding Strategy

Have students use the Decoding Big Words Strategy on page 14 to decode the following words:

witnesses, problematic, suddenly, admitted, pigmentation

Remind them to look for closed syllables in Step 3 of the strategy.

 Teacher-to-Teacher

Syllabication Rules: The following are two reliable syllabication rules:

- When two or more consonants appear together in the middle of a word, divide the word between them (e.g., lit/tle). Then try the short vowel sound. Note that this does not work if the consonants form a digraph such as *ch*, *tch*, *ck*, *ph*, *sh*, or *th*.
- When only one consonant appears between two vowels, divide the word before the consonant (e.g., ho/tel). Then try the long vowel sound.

Name _____ Date _____

Closed Syllables What's My Word?

1. Read each clue.

2. Look at the incomplete word.

3. Write the missing letters to solve the clue.

(1) You write with this.   p ___ n ___ ___ l

(2) If you miss a day of school, you are _____ .   a b ___ ___ ___ t

(3) Some bags are made of this.   p l ___ ___ ___ i c

(4) This animal likes to hop.   ___ ___ b b ___ ___

(5) If you see a crime committed, you are a _____ .   w ___ ___ n e s___

(6) This is a prickly plant.   ___ a c ___ u s

(7) This doctor checks your teeth.   ___ ___ n t ___ ___ ___

(8) This is the opposite of "entrance."   ___ ___ ___ t

(9) You wear these on your hands in winter.   ___ ___ t t ___ ___ s

(10) This word part can be found at the end of a word.   ___ u ___ ___ ___ x

Name _____ Date _____

Closed Syllable Speed Drill

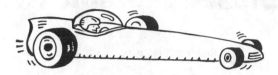

1. Draw a line between the closed syllables in each word.
2. Pronounce each word with your teacher.
3. Practice reading the words on your own.
4. When you are ready, have a partner time you reading the words for one minute. Keep practicing to improve your speed.

napkin	velvet	pumpkin	tactic	submit	hidden	cosmic	lesson	metric	contact
admit	absent	insect	kingdom	gossip	helmet	pencil	suspect	index	campus
metric	pumpkin	submit	absent	cosmic	gossip	velvet	hidden	kingdom	lesson
pencil	admit	helmet	napkin	pumpkin	helmet	admit	pencil	insect	submit
contact	tactic	metric	suspect	absent	velvet	lesson	gossip	metric	pumpkin
index	suspect	campus	cosmic	admit	index	tactic	hidden	campus	gossip
kingdom	velvet	insect	absent	lesson	napkin	insect	admit	velvet	contact
tactic	lesson	hidden	gossip	campus	submit	hidden	metric	index	pencil
helmet	cosmic	suspect	napkin	kingdom	campus	helmet	contact	kingdom	tactic
index	submit	insect	contact	pencil	pumpkin	absent	suspect	cosmic	napkin

	Words per Minute	Date	Partner
Timed Reading 1	_____	_____	_____
Timed Reading 2	_____	_____	_____
Timed Reading 3	_____	_____	_____

Name _____ Date _____

High-Frequency Syllable Fluency • Part 1

Read It

1. Underline the target syllable in each word.
2. Practice reading the words.
3. Cut apart the word cards.
4. See how fast you can sort the words by common syllable.

Syllables 11–20

e	election	**enormous**	**eliminate**
con	**contact**	**construct***	**concentration**
y	stormy	pushy	rubbery
ter	terrific	external	bitterly
ex	exit	**export**	**external**
al	colonial	memorial	territorial
de	**define**	**design**	decompose
com	**comment**	**complex**	**accommodate**
o	radio	rodeo	studio
di	diner	dilate	diversity

● For Part 2, make a copy of the reproducible on page 159 for each student.

Open Syllables Mini-lesson

Define

Tell students that an **open syllable** ends in a vowel. The vowel sound is generally long. For example, the first syllable in the word *local* (*lo*) ends in a vowel and has the long *o* vowel sound.

STEP 2

Transition to Longer Words

Help students transition from reading one-syllable to multisyllabic words. Have them read the open syllable in the first column, then use that syllable to read the word in the second column.

la	lazy
co	coma
pre	prefix
hi	hibernate
na	native
so	solo
ro	rotation
mo	momentary
me	meteor
fla	flavorful

STEP 3

Build Words

Write the following word parts on the board in random order:

> *ba, lo, la, do, sic, gel, bel, sin, dy, zy,*
> *cal, cate, cust, nate, nor, nut*

Have student pairs combine the word parts to build as many words as possible. These and other words can be formed:

> *basic, bagel, basin, local, locate, locust,*
> *label, lady, lazy, donate, donor, donut*

STEP 4

Apply Decoding Strategy

Have students use the Decoding Big Words Strategy to decode the following words:

> *probation, grocery, fatalistic, graciously,*
> *donations*

Remind them to look for open syllables in Step 3 of the strategy.

 Teacher-to-Teacher

Scoop and Code Syllables: On a reproducible master, write 20 multisyllabic words from an upcoming story. Have students work with a partner to draw an arc, or to scoop with their finger, under each syllable as they read each word aloud. Then have students code each syllable by syllable type (e.g., draw a macron over all open syllables with long vowel sounds, circle all the prefixes). *tāble*

Name _____ Date _____

Open Syllables Crossword Puzzle

1. Read the puzzle clues.
2. To answer each clue, select from the words in the box.
3. Write the correct word in the puzzle.

| lazy | prefix | solo | hibernate | grocery | donate | zebra | lethal | frequent | locate |

Across

3. deadly
5. to find
7. to give, as in a charity
8. food product you buy at a store
9. occurring a lot

Down

1. alone; by yourself
2. animal with black and white stripes
4. to sleep all winter
5. not eager to do work
6. word part that comes before a base word

Name _____ Date _____

Open Syllable Speed Drill

1. Underline the first syllable (the open syllable) in each word.
2. Pronounce each word with your teacher.
3. Practice reading the words on your own.
4. When you are ready, have a partner time you reading the words for one minute. Keep practicing to improve your speed.

agent	grocery	nature	mutate	cedar	vacant	tribal	donate	vocal	fatal
frequent	fragrant	senile	crisis	decent	lethal	gracious	zebra	museum	humid
donate	decent	agent	frequent	fragrant	grocery	fatal	humid	tribal	cedar
mutate	museum	crisis	vocal	vacant	zebra	nature	gracious	senile	museum
lethal	fragrant	donate	humid	frequent	agent	decent	cedar	humid	tribal
fatal	zebra	grocery	gracious	donate	fragrant	tribal	crisis	vacant	zebra
frequent	vacant	lethal	cedar	nature	vocal	museum	mutate	gracious	senile
lethal	gracious	tribal	vocal	senile	grocery	crisis	donate	decent	agent
grocery	crisis	fatal	nature	frequent	museum	mutate	zebra	lethal	humid
senile	cedar	mutate	decent	agent	fragrant	vacant	vocal	nature	fatal

	Words per Minute	Date	Partner
Timed Reading 1	_____	_____	_____
Timed Reading 2	_____	_____	_____
Timed Reading 3	_____	_____	_____

Name _____ Date _____

High-Frequency Syllable Fluency • Part 1

 Read It

1. Underline the target syllable in each word.
2. Practice reading the words.
3. Cut apart the word cards.
4. See how fast you can sort the words by common syllable.

Syllables 21–30

en	energy	enforce	environment
an	answer	anticipate	analyze
ty	property	priority	authority
ry	furry	summary	carry
u	uniform	unique	unify
ti	title	tiger	tidy
ri	rifle	rival	riot
be	become	believe	on behalf
per	percent	persist	perspective
to	total	tofu	totem pole

● For Part 2, make a copy of the reproducible on page 159 for each student.

Prefixes Mini-lesson *(un-, re-, in-/im-/ir-/il-)*

STEP 1

Define

Tell students that a **prefix** is a group of letters added to the beginning of a base word to make a new word. The prefix changes the word's meaning. Recognizing common prefixes can help students decode a word and figure out its meaning. For example, the word *unhappy* begins with the prefix *un-*. The prefix *un-* means "not" or "the opposite of." So, someone who is unhappy is <u>not</u> happy. Point out the following prefixes:

- **un-** means "not" or "the opposite of"

    The little girl was *unhappy* when her balloon popped.

    We need the key to *unlock* the safe.

- **re-** means "again" or "back/backwards"

    That villain will likely *reappear* on screen later in the movie.

    We had to *return* the movie the following week.

- **in-, im-, ir-, il-** mean "not" or "the opposite of" or "lack of"

    It is *inappropriate* to talk in class during an exam.

    Was it *impossible* to climb that mountain?

    Her decision to run for class president was *irreversible*.

    It is *illegal* to drive without a license.

STEP 2

Transition to Longer Words

Help students transition from reading one-syllable words to multisyllabic words. Have them read the prefix in the first column, then underline the prefix in the word in the second column. Guide students in reading the longer word and determining its meaning using the prefix.

un	unable
un	untie
un	unnecessary
re	reappear
re	remake
in	inappropriate
in	inaccessible
im	immature
ir	irresponsible
il	illogical

STEP 3

Build Words

Write the following word parts on the board:

un, re, in, im, ir, il, do, make, side, legal, mature, replace, able

Have student pairs combine the word parts to build as many words as possible. These and other words can be formed:

undo, redo, unable, remake, inside, illegal, immature, irreplaceable

STEP 4

Apply Decoding Strategy

Have students use the Decoding Big Words Strategy to decode the following words:

inexpensive, immortal, illiterate, reconstructed, unbelievable

Remind them to look for open syllables in Step 1 of the strategy.

Name _____ Date _____

Prefixes Prefix or Pretender? (*un-, re-, in-/im-/ir-/il-*)

1. Read each word pair.
2. Put an X over the word in each pair that does NOT begin with a prefix. Remember, after the prefix is removed, a base word must remain.

(1) unlikely   uncle   (7) under   unfold

(2) rebuild   realize   (8) restful   reunite

(3) indicate   inexpensive   (9) inches   indirect

(4) improper   important   (10) impatient   impala

(5) iron   irregular   (11) irresponsible   Iroquois

(6) illegal   illustrate   (12) illusion   illogical

Write sentences using one or more of the prefixed words above.

(13) _____

_____

_____

(14) _____

_____

_____

(15) _____

_____

_____

Name _____ Date _____

Prefix Speed Drill (*un-, re-, in-/im-/ir-/il-*)

1. Underline the prefix that begins each word.
2. Pronounce each word with your teacher.
3. Practice reading the words on your own.
4. When you are ready, have a partner time you reading the words for one minute. Keep practicing to improve your speed.

unable	reappear	impossible	incomplete	irregular	illegal	unequal	uncomfortable	reboot	immortal
indirect	irresponsible	illiterate	uneasy	reelect	improper	insane	irresistible	illogical	retrace
impossible	reboot	illogical	irregular	irresponsible	immortal	uncomfortable	reelect	uneasy	unequal
reappear	illiterate	indirect	retrace	incomplete	irresistible	illegal	improper	reelect	uneasy
insane	unable	retrace	uncomfortable	irresistible	reboot	impossible	unequal	immortal	irregular
irregular	improper	reappear	reelect	unequal	irresponsible	illogical	indirect	insane	incomplete
reboot	uncomfortable	uneasy	unable	illegal	indirect	immortal	retrace	irresponsible	improper
incomplete	insane	impossible	retrace	illiterate	reappear	illogical	uneasy	incomplete	reboot
illiterate	immortal	irresistible	illegal	reelect	illiterate	unable	indirect	illogical	impossible
unequal	irresistible	irregular	insane	uncomfortable	illegal	improper	irresponsible	unable	reappear

	Words per Minute	Date	Partner
Timed Reading 1	_____	_____	_____
Timed Reading 2	_____	_____	_____
Timed Reading 3	_____	_____	_____

Name _____ Date _____

High-Frequency Syllable Fluency • Part 1

 Read It

1. Underline the target syllable in each word.
2. Practice reading the words.
3. Cut apart the word cards.
4. See how fast you can sort the words by common syllable.

Syllables 31–40

pro	protect	**professional**	**prohibit**
ac	accuse	**acquire**	accidental*
ad	**adjust**	**advocate**	**adequate**
ar	argue	architect	**arbitrary**
ers	cleaners	bankers	gardeners
ment	treatment	**document**	**complement**
or	order	organ	**orientation**
tions	definitions	traditions	abbreviations
ble	table	**flexible**	**visible**
der	wonderful	derby	**derive**

• For Part 2, make a copy of the reproducible on page 159 for each student.

Suffixes Mini-lesson (*-s/-es, -ed, -ing*)

STEP 1

Define

Tell students that a **suffix** is a letter or group of letters added to the end of a base word. A suffix changes the word's meaning and often its part of speech. For example, the suffix *-ed* is added to the word *depart* (*departed*) to indicate that the action happened in the past. Point out the following suffixes:

- **-s/-es** used to make a word plural (The letters *-es* are often used when a word ends in *ch, tch, sh, ss, zz, x*.)
  The *bugs* were all over the tree.
  We went to several *beaches* in Thailand.

- **-ed** used to make verbs past tense (The *-ed* can have one of three sounds: /d/, /t/, or /ed/.)
  I carefully *closed* my book.
  I *placed* two plates on the table.
  I have never *acted* in a play.

- **-ing** verb form, present participle (When adding *-ing* to a CVC word, you must double the final consonant. When adding *-ing* to a word ending in *e*, you must drop the *e*.)
  We are *painting* pictures for the show.
  I like *running* in the mornings.
  We went *racing* across the gymnasium.

STEP 2

Transition to Longer Words

Help students transition from reading one-syllable to multisyllabic words. Have them read the word in the first column, then underline the suffix in the second column and read the longer word.

boy	boys
globe	globes
glass	glasses
watch	watches
squint	squinted
phone	phoned
trace	tracing
cover	covering

STEP 3

Build Words

Write the following base words on the board:

> *catch, miss, bag, line, drift, inch*

Have student pairs add the suffixes *-s, -es, -ed,* and *-ing* to build words. Ask them to check the dictionary to confirm spellings.

STEP 4

Apply Decoding Strategy

Have students use the Decoding Big Words Strategy to decode the following words:

> *reacting, guessing, conditioning, remembering, hibernating*

Remind them to look for suffixes in Step 2 of the strategy.

Name _____ Date _____

Suffixes Build-a-Word (-s/-es, -ed, -ing)

1. Add each suffix to the base word to form new words.

2. Check your spelling using a dictionary. Remember that when a word ends in the letter *e*, the *e* is dropped before adding *-ed* or *-ing*. Also, you need to double the final letter when adding a suffix to some words.

base word	-s	-ed	-ing
plant			
stop			
blame			
stay			
rhyme			

base word	-es	-ed	-ing
watch			
brush			
dress			
touch			
quiz			

Name _____ Date _____

Suffix Speed Drill

1. Underline the suffix in each word.
2. Pronounce each word with your teacher.
3. Practice reading the words on your own.
4. When you are ready, have a partner time you reading the words for one minute. Keep practicing to improve your speed.

masks	brushes	planned	catching	dreams	watches	prompted	speaking	globes	glasses
phoned	draining	skunks	inches	tempted	fixing	chains	splashes	spliced	waiting
prompted	masks	phoned	planned	globes	inches	watches	tempted	speaking	glasses
catching	tempted	dreams	skunks	brushes	waiting	phoned	chains	fixing	catching
spliced	draining	globes	glasses	planned	dreams	spliced	splashes	watches	fixing
brushes	splashes	prompted	masks	splashes	skunks	prompted	dreams	waiting	brushes
globes	catching	draining	glasses	inches	planned	chains	tempted	speaking	phoned
tempted	spliced	brushes	waiting	watches	chains	planned	globes	chains	prompted
watches	inches	spliced	draining	waiting	dreams	masks	skunks	speaking	fixing
phoned	glasses	splashes	catching	inches	draining	fixing	masks	skunks	speaking

	Words per Minute	Date	Partner
Timed Reading 1	_____	_____	_____
Timed Reading 2	_____	_____	_____
Timed Reading 3	_____	_____	_____

Name _____ Date _____

High-Frequency Syllable Fluency • Part 1

 Read It

1. Underline the target syllable in each word.
2. Practice reading the words.
3. Cut apart the word cards.
4. See how fast you can sort the words by common syllable.

Syllables 41–50

ma	maple	**major**	maniac
na	navy	nation	native
si	silent	silo	siren
un	under	uneven	unforgettable
at	atlas	**attitude**	**attach**
dis	**display**	**distribute**	**distort**
ca	cable	catering	Cajun
cal	calendar	calorie	calculate
man	mansion	**manual**	manuscript
ap	apple	application	apparatus

● For Part 2, make a copy of the reproducible on page 159 for each student.

Greek Roots and Combining Forms
Mini-lesson *(auto, bio, graph, hydro, meter)*

 STEP 1

Define

Tell students that a **root** is a basic word part that gives a word the most important part of its meaning. Many English words have roots from Greek, the language of the people from ancient Greece. Sometimes Greek roots are combined to form larger words. For example, the Greek roots *auto* and *graph* are used to form the word *autograph*. Teach the meanings of the following Greek roots and combining forms:

- **auto** means "self"
  The movie star signed *autographs* for his fans.

- **bio** means "life"
  Our class read a *biography* of Ben Franklin.

- **graph** means "written down, drawn, described, or recorded"
  Mrs. Rodriguez took a *photograph* of our class.

- **hydro** means "water"
  The runners needed more water because so many were becoming *dehydrated*.

- **meter** means "measure"
  We use a *speedometer* to measure how fast a car goes.

 STEP 2

Transition to Longer Words

Help students transition from reading one-syllable to multisyllabic words. Have them read the Greek root or combining form in the first column, then use that word part to read the multisyllabic word in the second column and determine its meaning. Model as needed.

auto	autograph
bio	biography
graph	graphics
hydro	hydrogen
meter	centimeter
auto	automobile
bio	biology
graph	telegraph
hydro	hydrophobia
meter	thermometer

STEP 3

Build Words

Write the following word parts on the board:

auto, bio, graph, hydro, meter, logy, ic, tele, gen, thermo, milli, y

Have student pairs combine the word parts to build as many words as possible. These and other words can be formed:

autograph, biography, graphic, hydrogen, thermometer, millimeter

 STEP 4

Apply Decoding Strategy

Have students use the Decoding Big Words Strategy to decode the following words:

autobiography, geography, dehydration, perimeter, photographic

Remind them to look for Greek roots and combining forms in Step 3 of the strategy.

Name _____ Date _____

Greek Roots and Combining Forms B-I-N-G-O

1. Write one of the following words in each blank randomly on the B-I-N-G-O board:

autograph, automatic, automobile, biology, biography, autobiography, photograph, graph, graphics, fire hydrant, hydrogen, dehydration, thermometer, meters, perimeter

You may use a word more than once.

2. Mark each word on the board as your teacher calls it.

B	I	N	G	O
		FREE		

Name _____ Date _____

Greek Root and Combining Form
Speed Drill (auto, bio, graph, hydro, meter)

1. Underline the Greek root in each word.

2. Pronounce each word with your teacher.

3. Practice reading the words on your own.

4. When you are ready, have a partner time you reading the words for one minute.
Keep practicing to improve your speed.

autograph	biography	graphic	hydroelectric	thermometer	automatic	biology	telegraph	hydrophobia	perimeter
automobile	biosphere	photograph	hydrogen	speedometer	autobiography	biophysics	geography	hydroplane	hydrometer
biology	perimeter	automobile	autograph	photograph	graphic	hydrogen	hydroelectric	biophysics	hydrophobia
thermometer	hydrophobia	geography	biosphere	biography	speedometer	perimeter	autobiography	photograph	automatic
photograph	geography	biology	telegraph	speedometer	autograph	hydroplane	graphic	telegraph	biophysics
telegraph	hydrogen	thermometer	geography	biosphere	automatic	biography	hydroplane	automobile	photograph
biosphere	hydroelectric	hydrophobia	automatic	biology	hydroelectric	autobiography	autograph	biophysics	telegraph
speedometer	automobile	autobiography	thermometer	hydrometer	perimeter	hydroplane	biography	graphic	hydrometer
hydroelectric	automatic	biosphere	perimeter	hydrogen	hydrometer	biology	biophysics	hydroplane	autograph
hydrophobia	autobiography	hydrogen	geography	thermometer	hydrometer	speedometer	graphic	automobile	biography

	Words per Minute	Date	Partner
Timed Reading 1	_____	_____	_____
Timed Reading 2	_____	_____	_____
Timed Reading 3	_____	_____	_____

Name _____ Date _____

High-Frequency Syllable Fluency • Part 1

Read It

1. Underline the target syllable in each word.

2. Practice reading the words.

3. Cut apart the word cards.

4. See how fast you can sort the words by common syllable.

Syllables 51–60

po	polite	**potential**	repossess
sion	television	**tension**	**dimension**
vi	vibrate	vital	**violate**
el	elevator	**element**	eloquent
est	tallest	straightest	healthiest
la	lazy	**labeled**	**labor**
lar	larger	larva	dollar*
pa	paper	pastry	patience
ture	picture	**mature**	**structure**
for	forest	fortune	forbid

● For Part 2, make a copy of the reproducible on page 159 for each student.

Latin Roots Mini-lesson (*audi, dict, ject, port, rupt*)

STEP 1

Define

Tell students that a **root** is a basic word part that gives a word the most important part of its meaning. Many English words have roots from Latin, the language of the ancient Romans. For example, the Latin root *port* is used to form the word *portable*. The root *port* means "carried" or "moved." Something that is *portable* is easily moved from place to place. Teach the meanings of the following Latin roots:

- **audi** means "hearing"
  The *audience* listened to the concert in the *auditorium*.

- **dict** means "speech/say/speak"
  The weather forecaster *predicted* the terrible winter storm.

- **ject** means "to throw"
  Why did he *reject* our offer to help clean up?

- **port** means "to carry"
  The company *imports* fruit from South America to the United States.

- **rupt** means "to break"
  The pipe *ruptured*, filling the kitchen with water.

STEP 2

Transition to Longer Words

Help students transition from reading one-syllable to multisyllabic words. Have them read the Latin root in the first column, then use that word part to read the multisyllabic word in the second column and determine its meaning. Model as needed.

audi	audience
dict	predict
ject	reject
port	export
rupt	rupture
audi	audible
dict	dictator
ject	projection
port	transportation
rupt	interruption

STEP 3

Build Words

Write the following word parts on the board:

audi, dict, ject, port, rupt, ence, pre, re, e, able, ex, im, in, ure, dis

Have student pairs combine the word parts to build as many words as possible. These and other words can be formed:

audience, predict, reject, eject, portable, export, import, inject, rupture, disrupt

STEP 4

Apply Decoding Strategy

Have students use the Decoding Big Words Strategy to decode the following words:

inaudible, auditorium, contradict, objection, eruption

Remind them to look for Latin roots in Step 3 of the strategy.

Name _____ Date _____

Latin Roots Latin Dictionary (*audi, dict, ject, port, rupt*)

1. Using what you know about the Latin root *port*, write a definition for each word.
2. Work with a partner.
3. Look up the word in a dictionary.
4. Record the dictionary definition under your definition.

Word: portable

My Definition: _____

Dictionary Definition: _____

_____

Word: export

My Definition: _____

Dictionary Definition: _____

_____

Word: import

My Definition: _____

Dictionary Definition: _____

_____

Word: transportation

My Definition: _____

Dictionary Definition: _____

_____

Word: reporter

My Definition: _____

Dictionary Definition: _____

_____

Name _____ Date _____

Latin Root Speed Drill (*audi, dict, ject, port, rupt*)

1. Underline the Latin root in each word.
2. Pronounce each word with your teacher.
3. Practice reading the words on your own.
4. When you are ready, have a partner time you reading the words for one minute. Keep practicing to improve your speed.

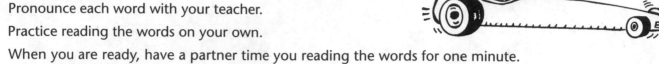

audience	dictate	reject	portable	rupture	audible	predict	projection	transportation	eruption
auditorium	contradict	eject	export	interrupt	audition	dictator	objection	reporter	disruption
dictate	audience	eruption	interrupt	reject	eject	rupture	projection	predict	audible
transportation	objection	contradict	portable	eject	auditorium	reject	dictator	interrupt	audition
eject	disruption	transportation	dictate	projection	predict	audition	audible	export	reporter
eruption	portable	disruption	audience	objection	rupture	contradict	auditorium	reporter	portable
reject	audible	predict	objection	audition	transportation	dictate	export	dictator	interrupt
projection	audition	portable	eruption	audience	disruption	interrupt	objection	auditorium	reporter
disruption	contradict	auditorium	eject	reporter	rupture	export	dictator	eruption	dictate
audible	reject	rupture	export	predict	dictator	audience	contradict	projection	transportation

	Words per Minute	Date	Partner
Timed Reading 1	_____	_____	_____
Timed Reading 2	_____	_____	_____
Timed Reading 3	_____	_____	_____

High-Frequency Syllable Fluency • Part 1

 Read It

1. Underline the target syllable in each word.
2. Practice reading the words.
3. Cut apart the word cards.
4. See how fast you can sort the words by common syllable.

Syllables 61–70

is	isn't	Islam	**issue***
mer	mercy	mercury	merchant
per	perfect	performance	**perceive**
ra	razor	radar	**ratio**
so	social	solar	isolation
ta	table	tablespoon	taper
as	aspirin*	**assume**	**assessment**
col	collect	**collapse**	collide
fi	**final**	**finance**	**finite**
ful	graceful	wonderful	doubtful

● For Part 2, make a copy of the reproducible on page 159 for each student.

Closed Syllables Mini-lesson

STEP 1

Define

Tell students that a **closed syllable** ends in a consonant. The vowel sound is generally short. For example, each syllable in the word *napkin* (*nap* and *kin*) ends in a consonant and has a short vowel sound.

STEP 2

Transition to Longer Words

Help students transition from reading one-syllable to multisyllabic words. Have them read the closed syllable in the first column, then use that syllable to read the multisyllabic word in the second column.

ab	absent
bud	budget
den	denim
fig	figment
in	insect
mag	magnet
pub	publishing
ran	randomly
splin	splinters
wit	witnesses

STEP 3

Build Words

Write the following word parts on the board:

> *in, can, den, pub, dex, let, sect, not, did,*
> *vas, yon, cer, tist, im, lish, lic*

Have student pairs use the word parts to build as many words as possible. These and other words can be formed:

> *index, inlet, insect, cannot, candid, cancer,*
> *canyon, dentist, denim, publish, public*

STEP 4

Apply Decoding Strategy

Have students use the Decoding Big Words Strategy to decode the following words:

> *customized, cancerous, fossilize, habitats,*
> *beverages*

Remind them to look for closed syllables in Step 3 of the strategy.

 **Teacher-to-Teacher**

Going From the Known to the Unknown: Teach syllabication strategies using known words, then provide ample opportunities for students to apply each strategy in context. For unknown words in the lesson, briefly state the word's meaning. List unknown words on the board for students to further explore during independent work time.

Name _____ Date _____

Closed Syllables Unscramble It!

1. Unscramble the letters to form words with closed syllables.

2. Write the words in the blank.

(1) tic   fan   tas   _____

(2) ment   im   prove   _____

(3) tat   i   hab   _____

(4) in   dent   pen   de   _____

(5) on   mel   er   wat   _____

(6) com   ly   mon   _____

(7) test   ant   con   _____

(8) ing   sip   gos   _____

(9) den   hid   un   _____

(10) ic   lem   at   prob   _____

Name _____ Date _____

Closed Syllable Speed Drill

1. Underline the closed syllable(s) in each word.
2. Pronounce each word with your teacher.
3. Practice reading the words on your own.
4. When you are ready, have a partner time you reading the words for one minute. Keep practicing to improve your speed.

picnic	contest	suddenly	summit	attic	pocket	denim	tantrum	dentist	princess
problematic	cabin	fabric	litmus	random	rapidly	figment	rustic	frantic	mishap
summit	frantic	denim	fabric	cabin	contest	attic	tantrum	suddenly	pocket
frantic	mishap	picnic	rapidly	litmus	rustic	random	attic	figment	dentist
mishap	summit	rustic	pocket	denim	tantrum	suddenly	litmus	dentist	princess
problematic	rapidly	fabric	picnic	summit	princess	figment	denim	frantic	pocket
rapidly	suddenly	tantrum	problematic	contest	random	attic	princess	cabin	frantic
fabric	random	attic	princess	figment	problematic	picnic	dentist	rustic	litmus
mishap	suddenly	figment	contest	tantrum	pocket	litmus	cabin	rapidly	picnic
contest	rustic	problematic	mishap	dentist	random	summit	fabric	denim	cabin

	Words per Minute	Date	Partner
Timed Reading 1	_____	_____	_____
Timed Reading 2	_____	_____	_____
Timed Reading 3	_____	_____	_____

Week-by-Week Phonics & Word Study Activities for the Intermediate Grades • © 2011 by Wiley Blevins • Scholastic Teaching Resources

Name _____ Date _____

High-Frequency Syllable Fluency • Part 1

Read It

1. Underline the target syllable in each word.
2. Practice reading the words.
3. Cut apart the word cards.
4. See how fast you can sort the words by common syllable.

Syllables 71–80

ger	danger	gerbil	germinate
low	below	lower	lowercase
ni	nitrogen	denial	alumni
par	**participate**	parcel	particle
son	person	reason	arson
tle	settle	gentle	belittle
day	daylight	Tuesday	Wednesday
ny	sunny	balcony	nylon*
pen	pencil	penalty	penetrate
pre	**predict**	**previous**	**precise**

● For Part 2, make a copy of the reproducible on page 159 for each student.

Open Syllables Mini-lesson

STEP 1

Define

Tell students that an **open syllable** ends in a vowel. The vowel sound is generally long. For example, the first syllable in the word *local* (*lo*) ends in a vowel and has the long *o* vowel sound.

STEP 2

Transition to Longer Words

Help students transition from reading one-syllable to multisyllabic words. Have them read the open syllable in the first column, then use that syllable to read the word in the second column.

ba	baby
di	diver
hi	hijacking
hu	human
so	social
fe	female
fra	fragrant
re	recently
va	vacancies
lo	location

STEP 3

Build Words

Write the following word parts on the board:

> *co, fa, mo, na, si, zy, lon, tal, vor, ment, tor, ture, vy, lent, lo, ren*

Have student pairs combine the word parts to build as many words as possible. These and other words can be formed:

> *cozy, colon, fatal, favor, moment, motor, nature, navy, silent, silo, siren*

STEP 4

Apply Decoding Strategy

Have students use the Decoding Big Words Strategy to decode the following words:

> *socialize, basically, illegally, reopening, secretive*

Remind them to look for open syllables in Step 3 of the strategy.

 Teacher-to-Teacher

Dictionaries: Use dictionaries with caution. Many dictionaries divide words according to how the word should be broken across lines. This sometimes has little to do with the division of the word into its syllables for the purpose of pronunciation.

Name _____ Date _____

Open Syllables Word Search

Find It

1. Find and circle the following words.
2. The words can be across, up and down, or on the diagonal. Some are written backwards.

| favorite | female | future | human | legal | lethal | locate | photo | recently | slogan | social | vital |

i	l	f	u	t	u	r	e	p	v
m	e	r	e	n	a	g	o	l	s
l	v	h	r	p	h	f	v	i	o
a	h	u	g	i	e	f	t	p	c
t	s	m	t	h	l	u	h	l	i
i	f	a	v	o	r	i	t	e	a
v	i	n	c	r	s	l	o	g	l
u	f	a	e	o	i	l	a	a	w
t	t	r	l	a	h	t	e	l	u
e	s	o	f	u	x	v	i	x	h
l	o	e	l	a	m	e	f	b	o
l	f	u	v	m	k	e	p	v	t
o	o	s	a	t	s	l	o	z	o
r	e	c	e	n	t	l	y	e	h
r	t	n	t	s	o	v	t	l	p

Name _____ Date _____

Open Syllable Speed Drill

1. Underline the open syllable (first syllable) in each word. Some words have more than one open syllable.
2. Pronounce each word with your teacher.
3. Practice reading the words on your own.
4. When you are ready, have a partner time you reading the words for one minute. Keep practicing to improve your speed.

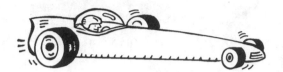

bacon	ozone	irate	slogan	photo	oval	soloist	sinus	equal	spinal
legal	favorite	female	primate	locate	major	minus	future	rodent	vital
photo	irate	legal	oval	favorite	primate	bacon	equal	locate	soloist
female	rodent	soloist	sinus	slogan	spinal	vital	favorite	future	major
ozone	oval	rodent	major	irate	minus	photo	vital	primate	slogan
sinus	future	ozone	female	legal	rodent	locate	bacon	major	equal
legal	soloist	primate	spinal	sinus	equal	irate	minus	female	future
vital	spinal	oval	locate	ozone	bacon	favorite	slogan	legal	photo
soloist	major	irate	female	photo	rodent	minus	ozone	oval	vital
slogan	locate	equal	favorite	minus	sinus	primate	spinal	future	bacon

	Words per Minute	Date	Partner
Timed Reading 1	_____	_____	_____
Timed Reading 2	_____	_____	_____
Timed Reading 3	_____	_____	_____

 Week-by-Week Phonics & Word Study Activities for the Intermediate Grades • © 2011 by Wiley Blevins • Scholastic Teaching Resources

Name _____ Date _____

High-Frequency Syllable Fluency • Part 1

 Read It

1. Underline the target syllable in each word.
2. Practice reading the words.
3. Cut apart the word cards.
4. See how fast you can sort the words by common syllable.

Syllables 81–90

tive	captive	**objective**	representative
car	cartoon	cargo	carbohydrate
ci	cider	citation	accidental*
mo	motion	mobile	**motive**
on	online	**ongoing**	onomatopoeia
ous	joyous	**obvious**	**ambiguous**
pi	pilot	pioneer	pious
se	secret	**sequence**	sequel
ten	tennis	tender	tenant
tor	torture	**monitor**	tortoise

● For Part 2, make a copy of the reproducible on page 159 for each student.

Review and Assess

Assessment Directions

1. Make one copy of the Real Word Test (page 54) and the Nonsense Word Test (page 55). You may wish to make the copy on cardstock for greater durability.

2. Make one copy of the Assessment Scoring Sheet (page 53) for each student.

3. Assess students individually. Have each student read the words from the Real Word Test, then the Nonsense Word Test.

4. Place a checkmark (✓) in the second column of the Assessment Scoring Sheet for each word read correctly. If the student correctly reads the word, but does so in a slow, labored manner, place a check minus (✓–) in the second column to indicate that fluency (automaticity with the sound-spellings) may still be an issue.

5. If the student incorrectly reads the word, record his or her attempt. Analyze the errors to notice patterns of difficulty. For example, some students might be overrelying on the initial letters in a word and not fully analyzing it. Other students might have difficulties with one specific aspect of the word, such as a complex spelling pattern. This analysis will inform the next steps you take to address these issues. During small-group instructional time, continue working with students on those skills not mastered.

6. Tally the scores from both tests. Students should be able to read the words with a minimum of 80% accuracy (i.e., 24 correct out of 30).

7. Create an Action Plan for students who struggle with specific skills (accuracy or speed issues) or students who fall below the 80% level. These students will need additional instruction, practice, and review on the skills covered in the lessons.

Assessment Scoring Sheet

Place a checkmark (✔) in the second column if the student reads the word correctly. If the student correctly reads the word but does so in a slow, labored manner, place a check minus (✔–) in the second column. If the student reads the word incorrectly, record his or her attempt.

Student Name: _____

Date: _____

Real Word Test	
1. suspect	
2. museum	
3. indirect	
4. prompted	
5. autograph	
6. portable	
7. random	
8. slogan	
9. interrupt	
10. hydrogen	
11. dentist	
12. unable	
13. reappear	
14. covering	
15. thermometer	
16. rejection	
17. witnesses	
18. locate	
19. predicted	
20. telegraph	

Nonsense Word Test	
1. rigfab	
2. napzeb	
3. moku	
4. lofam	
5. pagbo	
6. lepsing	
7. zotted	
8. unflups	
9. premeff	
10. krubgraph	

Scores: _____ Real Word Test

_____ Nonsense Word Test

_____ Total Score

Fluency: ❑ Good

❑ Poor

Skills Needing Additional Work:

Action Plan:

Name _____ Date _____

Real Word Test

1.	suspect	11.	dentist
2.	museum	12.	unable
3.	indirect	13.	reappear
4.	prompted	14.	covering
5.	autograph	15.	thermometer
6.	portable	16.	rejection
7.	random	17.	witnesses
8.	slogan	18.	locate
9.	interrupt	19.	predicted
10.	hydrogen	20.	telegraph

Name _____ Date _____

Nonsense Word Test

1. rigfab

2. napzeb

3. moku

4. lofam

5. pagbo

6. lepsing

7. zotted

8. unflups

9. premeff

10. krubgraph

Consonant + *le* Syllables Mini-lesson

STEP 1

Define

Tell students that when a word ends in *le*, usually these letters and the consonant that comes before them form the last syllable. This is called a **consonant + *le* syllable**, or final stable syllable. For example, the final stable syllable in the word *table* is *ble*.

STEP 2

Transition to Longer Words

Help students transition from reading one-syllable to multisyllabic words. Have them read the simple word or syllable in the first column, then use that word or syllable to read the multisyllabic word in the second column. The left-hand set uses closed syllables; the right-hand set uses open syllables.

rub	rubble	fa	fable
un	uncle	ma	maple
can	candle	ca	cable
ruf	ruffle	cra	cradle
jig	jiggle	ti	title
dim	dimple	bi	bible
rat	rattle	bri	bridle
puz	puzzle	cy	cycle

STEP 3

Build Words

Write the following word parts on the board:

> *ble, gle, dle, tle, a, bub, drib, rum, un, bu, jun, jum, wig, mid, ped, pud, bat, bot, ket, man*

Have student pairs combine the word parts to build as many words as possible. These and other words can be formed:

> *able, bubble, dribble, rumble, unable, bugle, jungle, jumble, wiggle, middle, peddle, puddle, battle, bottle, kettle, mantle*

STEP 4

Apply Decoding Strategy

Have students use the Decoding Big Words Strategy to decode the following words:

> *incurable, quadruple, tabernacle, timetable, resembled*

Remind them to look for consonant + *le* syllables in Step 3 of the strategy.

 **Teacher-to-Teacher**

Final Stable Syllables: Other final stable syllables include -*tion*, -*sion*, -*ture*, and -*sure*. These syllables don't fall into one of the six Syllable Types, but should be formally taught due to their high frequency in English words.

Name _____ Date _____

Consonant + *le* Syllables What's My Word?

1. Read each clue.
2. Look at the incomplete word.
3. Write the missing letters to solve the clue.

(1) A yummy red fruit   a p ___ ___ ___

(2) A little laugh   g i g ___ ___ ___

(3) A story that teaches a moral or lesson   f a ___ ___ ___

(4) The national bird of the U.S.   e a ___ ___ ___

(5) In the center   m i d ___ ___ ___

(6) Not difficult or complicated   s i m ___ ___ ___

(7) Person married to your aunt   u n ___ ___ ___

(8) To move quickly back and forth   w i g ___ ___ ___

(9) A kind of bug   b e e ___ ___ ___

(10) More than one cow   c a t ___ ___ ___

Write your own clues below for a classmate to answer.

(11) _____   ___ ___ ___ ___ ___

(12) _____   ___ ___ ___ ___ ___

Name _____ Date _____

Consonant + *le* Syllable Speed Drill

1. Underline the consonant + *le* syllable at the end of each word.
2. Pronounce each word with your teacher.
3. Practice reading the words on your own.
4. When you are ready, have a partner time you reading the words for one minute. Keep practicing to improve your speed.

bubble	dribble	giggle	squiggle	huddle	riddle	temple	drizzle	vehicle	castle
cable	noble	bugle	bridle	maple	enable	timetable	eagle	needle	fable
squiggle	vehicle	cable	huddle	castle	noble	temple	riddle	drizzle	giggle
bugle	dribble	enable	bubble	bridle	huddle	maple	noble	vehicle	needle
enable	timetable	drizzle	eagle	dribble	bugle	cable	giggle	bridle	squiggle
riddle	castle	eagle	bugle	timetable	bubble	noble	bridle	temple	dribble
needle	enable	maple	huddle	fable	giggle	drizzle	cable	riddle	timetable
drizzle	eagle	squiggle	giggle	enable	dribble	bugle	noble	maple	vehicle
squiggle	castle	bubble	needle	cable	fable	riddle	temple	castle	fable
fable	needle	maple	vehicle	eagle	huddle	timetable	bridle	bubble	temple

	Words per Minute	Date	Partner
Timed Reading 1	_____	_____	_____
Timed Reading 2	_____	_____	_____
Timed Reading 3	_____	_____	_____

Name _____ Date _____

High-Frequency Syllable Fluency • Part 1

 Read It

1. Underline the target syllable in each word.
2. Practice reading the words.
3. Cut apart the word cards.
4. See how fast you can sort the words by common syllable.

Syllables 91–100

ver	vertical	**version**	verdict
ber	November	barber	limber
can	candle	cancer	cantaloupe
dy	candy	bodybuilder	**subsidy**
et	quiet	etcetera	etiquette
it	**edit**	**credit**	**exhibit**
mu	music	museum	**mutual**
no	noble	notion	**innovate**
ple	simple	**couple**	people
cu	cucumber	cupid	cuticle

● For Part 2, make a copy of the reproducible on page 159 for each student.

Vowel Team Syllables Mini-lesson

Define

Tell students that sometimes two or more letters together stand for one vowel sound, such as *ai*, *aw*, *ay*, *ea*, *ee*, *ew*, *igh*, *oa*, *ow*, *oo*, *oi*, *oy*, *ou*, *ie*, and *ei*. These letter pairs are called vowel teams. Since the letters are a team, they must stay together in the same syllable. This type of syllable is called a **vowel team syllable**. For example, the vowel team syllable in the word *mailbox* is *mail*. (Note: You might need to remind students that in some vowel spellings, consonants such as *y* and *w* act as vowels.)

STEP 2

Transition to Longer Words

Help students transition from reading one-syllable to multisyllabic words. Have them read the simple word in the first column, then use that word to read the multisyllabic word in the second column.

pay	paycheck
plain	explain
meal	oatmeal
sea	seaweed
free	freedom
spoil	spoilage
mail	mailbox

 **Teacher-to-Teacher**

book	handbook
peach	impeached
play	displaying

Build Words

Write the following word parts on the board:

re, under, over, paid, dis, play, way, half, head, hall, mis, treat, coat, rain, ground, camp, battle, fore

Have student pairs combine the word parts to build as many words as possible. These and other words can be formed:

repaid, underpaid, overpaid, display, replay, halfway, headway, hallway, mistreat, retreat, raincoat, overcoat, campground, battleground, foreground

Apply Decoding Strategy

Have students use the Decoding Big Words Strategy to decode the following words:

viewpoints, approaches, neighborhood, powerhouse, auctioneer

Remind them to look for vowel team syllables in Step 3 of the strategy.

Vowels and Consonants: You may need to review with students the difference between a vowel and a consonant. Some students haven't mastered this language of instruction, thereby making the discussion of syllables confusing. Adding to that confusion is the fact that in some vowel spellings, consonants act as vowels (e.g., *ay*, *ew*, *igh*, *ow*).

Week-by-Week Phonics & Word Study Activities for the Intermediate Grades • © 2011 by Wiley Blevins • Scholastic Teaching Resources

Name _____ Date _____

Vowel Team Syllables Crossword Puzzle

1. Read the puzzle clues.

2. To answer each clue, select from the words in the box.

3. Write the correct word in the puzzle.

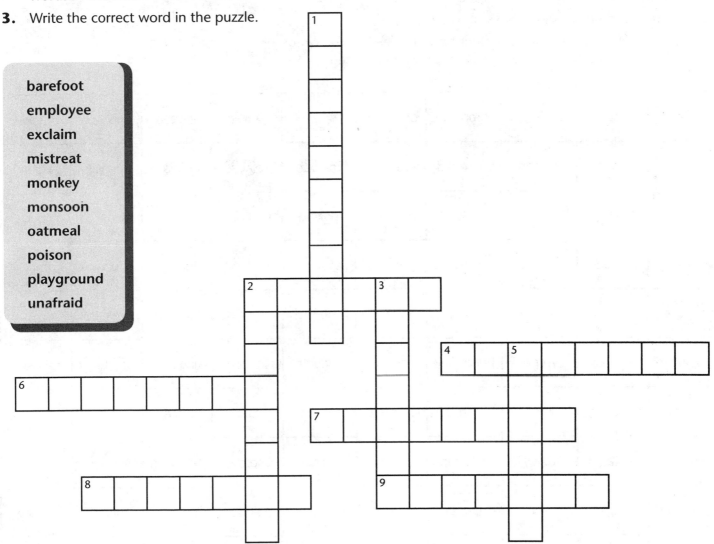

barefoot

employee

exclaim

mistreat

monkey

monsoon

oatmeal

poison

playground

unafraid

Across

2. an animal that can climb a tree

4. a worker

6. not wearing shoes

7. not scared

8. a breakfast food

9. a terrible wind and rain storm

Down

1. a place where children play

2. to treat badly

3. to say loudly

5. a deadly chemical

Name _____ Date _____

Vowel Team Syllable Speed Drill

1. Underline the vowel team (or teams) in each word. Remember that each vowel team must remain in the same syllable.
2. Pronounce each word with your teacher.
3. Practice reading the words on your own.
4. When you are ready, have a partner time you reading the words for one minute. Keep practicing to improve your speed.

amount	beneath	complain	compound	decaying	displayed	exclaim	indeed	mislead	monkey
oatmeal	handbook	poison	overpaid	raccoon	railroad	release	seesaw	unafraid	valley
complain	amount	release	mislead	decaying	poison	raccoon	monkey	seesaw	indeed
decaying	overpaid	oatmeal	compound	railroad	exclaim	displayed	beneath	raccoon	complain
release	handbook	exclaim	amount	poison	oatmeal	valley	railroad	indeed	seesaw
displayed	compound	overpaid	handbook	mislead	beneath	indeed	unafraid	complain	monkey
poison	release	mislead	indeed	overpaid	amount	valley	oatmeal	seesaw	railroad
exclaim	beneath	valley	compound	handbook	mislead	unafraid	decaying	monkey	raccoon
unafraid	complain	poison	release	displayed	handbook	compound	raccoon	oatmeal	seesaw
valley	unafraid	beneath	overpaid	railroad	exclaim	monkey	amount	displayed	decaying

	Words per Minute	Date	Partner
Timed Reading 1	_____	_____	_____
Timed Reading 2	_____	_____	_____
Timed Reading 3	_____	_____	_____

 Week-by-Week Phonics & Word Study Activities for the Intermediate Grades • © 2011 by Wiley Blevins • Scholastic Teaching Resources

Name _____ Date _____

High-Frequency Syllable Fluency • Part 1

 Read It

1. Underline the target syllable in each word.
2. Practice reading the words.
3. Cut apart the word cards.
4. See how fast you can sort the words by common syllable.

Syllables 101–110

fac	factory	**factor**	faculty
fer	**transfer**	ferocious	**differentiate**
gen	gentle	**gender**	**generation**
ic	**topic**	**classic**	**dynamic**
land	landmark	Iceland	landscape
'light	lightning	**highlight**	lightweight
ob	object	obvious	observation
of	often	office	offering
pos	possible	**positive**	posture
tain	**maintain**	**obtain**	**retain**

● For Part 2, make a copy of the reproducible on page 159 for each student.

Prefixes Mini-lesson *(dis-, em-/en-, non-)*

 STEP 1

Define

Tell students that a **prefix** is a group of letters added to the beginning of a base word to make a new word. The prefix changes the word's meaning. Recognizing common prefixes can help students decode a word and figure out its meaning. For example, the word *unhappy* begins with the prefix *un-*. The prefix *un-* means "not" or "the opposite of." So, someone who is unhappy is <u>not</u> happy. Point out the following prefixes:

- **dis-** means "not" or "the opposite of" or "lack of"

  We *disagreed* with the umpire's call in the game.

  It is important to carefully *disinfect* a hospital room.

  I was in *disbelief* at the ending to that mystery.

- **em-/en-** means "cause to"

  Grandma Shelby *embraced* her grandchildren at the airport.

  A passport will *enable* you to travel to many countries.

- **non-** means "not" or "lacking/without" (If the root word is a proper noun, *non-* is added with a hyphen, as in non-Catholic.)

  Make sure to use *nontoxic* crayons with young children.

  The thin lady always looked for *nonfat* foods and drinks.

STEP 2

Transition to Longer Words

Help students transition from reading one-syllable to multisyllabic words. Have them read the prefix in the first column, then use that prefix to read and define the multisyllabic word in the second column.

dis	disable
em	empower
en	enclose
non	nonstop
dis	disappear
em	embark
en	enjoy
non	nonfiction

 STEP 3

Build Words

Write the following word parts on the board:

dis, em, en, non, obey, like, color, able, roll, large, ploy, drip, stop, living

Have student pairs combine the word parts to build as many words as possible. These and other words can be formed:

disobey, dislike, discolor, disable, enable, enroll, enlarge, employ, nondrip, nonstop, nonliving

 STEP 4

Apply Decoding Strategy

Have students use the Decoding Big Words Strategy to decode the following words:

disconnected, enlighten, embattle, nonabrasive, nonliving

Remind them to look for prefixes in Step 1 of the strategy.

Name _____ Date _____

Prefixes Connect-a-Word (dis-, em-/en-, non-)

1. Select one word part from each column to make a new word. Each word part can be used only once.
2. Write the new word in the last column.

Column 1	Column 2	Column 3	Word Formed
dis	joy	est	
dis	fic	ic	
dis	ap	age	
em	tox	tion	
en	ploy	ed	
en	hon	pear	
non	a	ing	
non	cour	gree	

Name _____ Date _____

Prefix Speed Drill (*dis-, em-/en-, non-*)

1. Underline the prefix that begins each word
2. Pronounce each word with your teacher.
3. Practice reading the words on your own.
4. When you are ready, have a partner time you reading the words for one minute. Keep practicing to improve your speed.

disable	embark	enclose	nonliving	disagree	embattle	enable	nonspecific	displease	embedded
nonathletic	disapprove	embrace	encircle	nonstop	disqualify	enlarge	nonfiction	dislike	enrage
nonliving	enclose	nonathletic	disagree	encircle	enable	nonstop	displease	embark	enlarge
disqualify	embattle	nonfiction	embrace	disable	enlarge	nonspecific	nonfiction	disapprove	enable
embedded	nonliving	enclose	nonathletic	nonstop	disagree	embark	disable	dislike	encircle
disapprove	disqualify	enlarge	nonspecific	embrace	nonliving	enrage	nonathletic	displease	dislike
nonstop	embedded	embattle	disapprove	enclose	embrace	enable	embark	encircle	disagree
nonfiction	nonspecific	disqualify	embedded	enlarge	disable	dislike	displease	nonathletic	enrage
disagree	dislike	enable	nonstop	embattle	enrage	nonliving	encircle	disapprove	embrace
disqualify	displease	nonspecific	enclose	nonfiction	embedded	enrage	embattle	embark	disable

	Words per Minute	Date	Partner
Timed Reading 1	_____	_____	_____
Timed Reading 2	_____	_____	_____
Timed Reading 3	_____	_____	_____

Name _____ Date _____

High-Frequency Syllable Fluency • Part 1

Read It

1. Underline the target syllable in each word.
2. Practice reading the words.
3. Cut apart the word cards.
4. See how fast you can sort the words by common syllable.

Syllables 111–120

den	dentist	Denmark	**identical**
ings	spellings	carvings	belongings
mag	magnet	magazine	magnify
ments	moments	governments	**supplements**
set	settle	**offset**	setbacks
some	something	**somewhat**	somewhere
sub	subway	**substitute**	subterranean
sur	**survive**	**survey**	surgery
ters	**chapters**	**alters**	**encounters**
tu	**virtual**	**eventual**	**fluctuate**

● For Part 2, make a copy of the reproducible on page 159 for each student.

Suffixes Mini-lesson (-ly, -er/-or, -ion/-tion/-ation/-ition)

STEP 1

Define

Tell students that a **suffix** is a letter or group of letters added to the end of a base word. A suffix changes the word's meaning and often its part of speech. For example, the suffix -ed is added to the word *depart* (*departed*) to indicate that the action happened in the past. Point out the following suffixes:

- **-ly** used to show a "characteristic of" or "in the manner of"

  We *happily* went to the circus on Saturday.

- **-er/-or** used to show "a person connected with" or "one who"

  The *farmer* grew wheat and corn.

  The *sailor* was out to sea for a week.

- **-ion/-tion/-ation/-ition** used to show "act," "process," or "state of being" (This suffix turns a root word into a noun.)

  Participation in the blood drive was up 50 percent this year.

  There is great *confusion* about when the concert will start.

STEP 2

Transition to Longer Words

Help students transition from reading one-syllable to multisyllabic words. Have them read the suffix in the first column, then use that suffix to read the multisyllabic word in the second column.

ly	sadly	ly	happily
er	climber	er	dreamer
or	actor	or	visitor
ion	pollution	ation	declaration
tion	attention	ition	definition

STEP 3

Build Words

Write the following word parts on the board:

ion, attract, celebrate, calculate, digest, direct, express, motivate, reject, speculate

Have student pairs combine the word parts to build as many words as possible. Remind them that they might need to alter the spelling of a base word when adding the suffix. These and other words can be formed:

attraction, celebration, calculation, digestion, direction, expression, motivation, rejection, speculation

STEP 4

Apply Decoding Strategy

Have students use the Decoding Big Words Strategy to decode the following words:

abbreviation, expressionless, communication, investigators, conductor

Remind them to look for suffixes in Step 2 of the strategy.

💡 Teacher-to-Teacher

Spelling Changes: Work with students to master the spelling changes needed when adding -ion, -tion, -ation, or -ition. For example, the word *collide* drops the e, then changes the d to an s before adding *ion* to form *collision*.

Name _____ Date _____

Suffixes Build-a-Word (-ly, -er/-or, -ion/-tion/-ation/-ition)

1. Add one of the following suffixes to the base word to form new words: -ly, -er, -or, -ion, -tion, -ation, -ition.
2. Remember that spelling changes might be necessary.
3. Check the spelling using a dictionary.

Base Word	New Word(s) Formed
dream	
collect	
create	
sleep	
direct	
illustrate	
exhibit	
demonstrate	
subscribe	
collide	

Name _____ Date _____

Suffix Speed Drill (-ly, -er/-or, -ion/-tion/-ation/-ition)

1. Underline the suffix that ends each word.
2. Pronounce each word with your teacher.
3. Practice reading the words on your own.
4. When you are ready, have a partner time you reading the words for one minute. Keep practicing to improve your speed.

brightly	climber	addition	attention	correctly	advisor	concentration	digestion	quietly	governor
mansion	rotation	delicately	gardener	tradition	eruption	repeatedly	investigator	explosion	education
correctly	governor	attention	mansion	climber	delicately	quietly	concentration	eruption	addition
digestion	brightly	advisor	rotation	explosion	mansion	gardener	quietly	tradition	repeatedly
governor	investigator	delicately	advisor	digestion	concentration	climber	eruption	gardener	digestion
advisor	correctly	investigator	brightly	repeatedly	rotation	mansion	attention	addition	rotation
delicately	explosion	concentration	investigator	attention	tradition	eruption	climber	education	gardener
mansion	tradition	governor	correctly	repeatedly	brightly	explosion	rotation	digestion	quietly
concentration	addition	advisor	education	governor	investigator	correctly	education	gardener	explosion
repeatedly	delicately	tradition	addition	eruption	attention	education	quietly	climber	brightly

	Words per Minute	Date	Partner
Timed Reading 1	_____	_____	_____
Timed Reading 2	_____	_____	_____
Timed Reading 3	_____	_____	_____

Name _____ Date _____

High-Frequency Syllable Fluency • Part 1

Read It

1. Underline the target syllable in each word.
2. Practice reading the words.
3. Cut apart the word cards.
4. See how fast you can sort the words by common syllable.

Syllables 121–130

af	afternoon	African	affluent
au	**author**	autumn	**automate**
cy	fancy	**policy**	**currency**
fa	fable	favorite	fatal
im	important	**image**	**Immigrate**
li	lion	**license**	**intelligence***
lo	lotion	**locate**	**psychology**
men	mention	**mental**	fundamental
min	minute	**minimum**	**administrate**
mon	monster	monsoon	monument

● For Part 2, make a copy of the reproducible on page 159 for each student.

Greek Roots Mini-lesson (*ology, photo, scope, tele, therm*)

 STEP 1

Define

Tell students that a **root** is a basic word part that gives a word the most important part of its meaning. Many English words have roots from Greek, the language of the people from ancient Greece. Sometimes Greek roots are combined to form larger words. For example, the Greek roots *auto* and *graph* are used to form the word *autograph*. Teach the meanings of the following Greek roots and combining forms:

- **ology** means "idea, word, speech, or study of"
  We studied *geology* to learn about Earth and its many layers.

- **photo** means "light"
  Our class *photograph* is my favorite picture from last year.

- **scope** means "to see"
  The scientist used a *telescope* to see the newly discovered star.

- **tele** means "far away/distant"
  Did you buy the new *telephone* with wireless Internet?

- **therm** means "heat"
  What temperature does the thermometer show today?

 STEP 2

Transition to Longer Words

Help students transition from reading one-syllable to multisyllabic words. Have them read the Greek root in the first column, then use that root to read and define the multisyllabic word in the second column.

ology	biology
photo	photograph

scope	telescope
tele	telephone
therm	thermos
ology	zoology
photo	photosynthesis
scope	microscope
tele	television
therm	thermometer

 STEP 3

Build Words

Write the following word parts on the board:

tele, scope, logy, phone, vision, micro, graph, geo, zoo, bio

Have student pairs combine the word parts to build as many words as possible. These and other words can be formed:

telescope, telephone, television, telegraph, microscope, microphone, geology, zoology, biology

STEP 4

Apply Decoding Strategy

Have students use the Decoding Big Words Strategy to decode the following words:

meteorology, photogenic, stethoscope, telegraphic, thermostat

Remind them to look for Greek roots in Step 3 of the strategy.

Name _____ Date _____

Greek Roots B-I-N-G-O *(ology, photo, scope, tele, therm)*

1. Write one of the following words randomly in each blank on the B-I-N-G-O board:

*geology, biology, meteorology, photography, photocopy, photosynthesis, telescope,
microscope, stethoscope, telephone, television, thermos*

You may use a word more than once.

2. Mark each word on the board as your teacher calls it.

B	I	N	G	O
		FREE		

Name _____ Date _____

Greek Root Speed Drill *(ology, photo, scope, tele, therm)*

1. Underline the Greek root in each word.
2. Pronounce each word with your teacher.
3. Practice reading the words on your own.
4. When you are ready, have a partner time you reading the words for one minute.
   Keep practicing to improve your speed.

geology	photography	telescope	telephone	thermos	biology	photocopy	microscope	telepathy	thermostat
meteorology	photogenic	periscope	telegraph	thermal	theology	photosynthesis	stethoscope	television	thermometer
photography	telephone	meteorology	biology	telescope	thermos	telegraph	microscope	photocopy	telepathy
photocopy	photosynthesis	photogenic	geology	thermostat	periscope	biology	television	theology	thermos
telephone	thermal	microscope	thermometer	stethoscope	geology	periscope	photography	telepathy	television
photosynthesis	meteorology	stethoscope	telescope	photogenic	thermostat	telegraph	theology	thermal	telescope
microscope	photocopy	telephone	photography	thermal	thermos	thermometer	geology	telegraph	periscope
stethoscope	telescope	photosynthesis	thermos	theology	biology	thermostat	thermometer	television	telepathy
thermal	microscope	thermostat	photocopy	photography	stethoscope	photogenic	telegraph	geology	thermometer
telepathy	theology	thermos	meteorology	biology	periscope	photosynthesis	meteorology	television	photogenic

	Words per Minute	Date	Partner
Timed Reading 1	_____	_____	_____
Timed Reading 2	_____	_____	_____
Timed Reading 3	_____	_____	_____

Week-by-Week Phonics & Word Study Activities for the Intermediate Grades • © 2011 by Wiley Blevins • Scholastic Teaching Resources

Name _____ Date _____

High-Frequency Syllable Fluency • Part 1

 Read It

1. Underline the target syllable in each word.
2. Practice reading the words.
3. Cut apart the word cards.
4. See how fast you can sort the words by common syllable.

Syllables 131–140

op	**option**	**cooperate**	optical
out	outside	**outcome**	**output**
rec	record	recognize	recreation
ro	robot	rotate	robust
sen	sentence	Senate	sensible
side	sidewalk	sideline	**reside***
tal	talent	tally	talon
tic	arctic	scholastic	**domestic**
ties	abilities	properties	treaties
ward	upward	westward	**straightforward**

● For Part 2, make a copy of the reproducible on page 159 for each student.

Latin Roots Mini-lesson (scrib/script, spect, struct, tract, vis)

STEP 1

Define

Tell students that a **root** is a basic word part that gives a word the most important part of its meaning. Many English words have roots from Latin, the language of the ancient Romans. For example, the Latin root *port* is used to form the word *portable*. The root *port* means "carried" or "moved." Something that is *portable* is easily moved from place to place. Teach the meanings of the following Latin roots:

- **scrib/script** means "writing"

  The author turned in his *manuscript* for his next book on time!

- **spect** means "to look at"

  We need to *inspect* the delivery to make sure everything arrived.

- **struct** means "build"

  They *constructed* a large building on the corner of our street.

- **tract** means "to draw or pull"

  The farmer used a *tractor* to move the hay to the barn.

- **vis** means "sight or seeing"

  We try to *visualize* what we are reading to better understand it.

STEP 2

Transition to Longer Words

Help students transition from reading one-syllable to multisyllabic words. Have them read the Latin root in the first column, then use that root to read and define the multisyllabic word in the second column. Model as needed.

script	description
spect	inspect

struct	construct
tract	tractor
vis	visitor
scrib	scribble
spect	spectator
struct	destruction
tract	subtraction
vis	invisible

STEP 3

Build Words

Write the following word parts on the board:

> *tract, vis, struct, spect, in, or, re, con, ion, ex, it*

Have student pairs combine the word parts to build as many words as possible. These and other words can be formed:

> *tractor, traction, extract, vision, visit, instruct, instruction, construct, construction, inspect, inspector, respect, inspection, extract*

STEP 4

Apply Decoding Strategy

Have students use the Decoding Big Words Strategy to decode the following words:

> *inscription, spectacular, reconstruction, attractive, supervisor*

Remind them to look for Latin roots in Step 3 of the strategy.

Name _____ Date _____

Latin Roots Dictionary (*scrib/script, spect, struct, tract, vis*)

1. Using what you know about the Latin roots, write a definition for each word.
2. Work with a partner.
3. Look up the word in a dictionary.
4. Record the dictionary definition under your definition.

Word: invisible

My Definition: _____

Dictionary Definition: _____

_____

Word: manuscript

My Definition: _____

Dictionary Definition: _____

_____

Word: spectator

My Definition: _____

Dictionary Definition: _____

_____

Word: inspector

My Definition: _____

Dictionary Definition: _____

_____

Word: construct

My Definition: _____

Dictionary Definition: _____

_____

Name _____ Date _____

Latin Root Speed Drill (scrib/script, spect, struct, tract, vis)

1. Underline the Latin root in each word.
2. Pronounce each word with your teacher.
3. Practice reading the words on your own.
4. When you are ready, have a partner time you reading the words for one minute.
   Keep practicing to improve your speed.

describe	transcript	inspect	instruct	tractor	vision	manuscript	scribe	spectacle	destruction
attract	visual	scribble	description	spectator	construction	attractive	subtraction	invisible	visualize
transcript	spectacle	invisible	visual	inspect	description	scribe	vision	construction	tractor
spectacle	manuscript	describe	attract	instruct	scribble	destruction	subtraction	tractor	spectator
inspect	construction	attract	invisible	construction	attractive	vision	instruct	description	scribe
manuscript	spectator	transcript	attractive	describe	visualize	scribble	tractor	subtraction	visualize
construction	visual	inspect	vision	attractive	destruction	subtraction	scribe	scribble	instruct
destruction	visualize	manuscript	spectacle	scribe	transcript	attract	invisible	attractive	subtraction
visualize	vision	spectator	describe	visual	spectacle	description	instruct	attract	inspect
visual	destruction	invisible	description	manuscript	transcript	spectator	scribble	tractor	describe

	Words per Minute	Date	Partner
Timed Reading 1	_____	_____	_____
Timed Reading 2	_____	_____	_____
Timed Reading 3	_____	_____	_____

Name _____ Date _____

High-Frequency Syllable Fluency • Part 1

Read It

1. Underline the target syllable in each word.
2. Practice reading the words.
3. Cut apart the word cards.
4. See how fast you can sort the words by common syllable.

Syllables 141–150

age	ageless	agelessness	voyage*
ba	bacon	baby-sitter	basic
but	butter	button	rebuttal
cit	citizen	citrus	**explicit**
cle	**cycle**	uncle	**vehicle**
co	coconut	**coordination**	**coincide**
cov	cover	recovered	covet
da	David	**data**	**foundation**
dif	different	difficult	differentiate
ence	excellence	difference	obedience

● For Part 2, make a copy of the reproducible on page 159 for each student.

Week 17

Consonant + *le* **Syllables** Mini-lesson

STEP 1

Define

Tell students that when a word ends in *le*, usually these letters and the consonant that comes before them form the last syllable. This is called a **consonant + *le* syllable**, or final stable syllable. For example, the final stable syllable in the word *table* is *ble*.

STEP 2

Transition to Longer Words

Help students transition from reading one-syllable to multisyllabic words. Have them read the consonant plus *le* syllable in the first column, then use that syllable to read the multisyllabic word in the second column.

ble	dribble
cle	circle
dle	dwindle
fle	shuffle
gle	squiggle
ple	sample
tle	Seattle
zle	drizzle

STEP 3

Build Words

Write the following word parts on the board in random order:

> *ble, cle, dle, fle, gle, ple, tle, zle, fa, no, un, pud, ruf, gig, jug, dim, rip, lit, cat, fiz*

Have student pairs use the word parts to build as many words as possible. These and other words can be formed:

> *fable, noble, uncle, puddle, ruffle, giggle, juggle, dimple, ripple, little, cattle, fizzle*

STEP 4

Apply Decoding Strategy

Have students use the Decoding Big Words Strategy to decode the following words:

> *durable, comprehensible, skedaddle, periwinkle, reassemble*

Remind them to look for consonant + *le* syllables in Step 3 of the strategy.

 Teacher-to-Teacher

Stable Syllables: Consonant + *le* and Consonant + *re* are two very stable syllables in English.

Name _____ Date _____

Consonant + *le* Syllables Word Search

Find It

1. Find and circle the following words.

2. The words can be across, up and down, or on the diagonal. Some are written backwards.

| assemble | durable | purple | noodle | bundle | puzzle | vehicle | bottle | brittle | title |

n	b	r	i	t	z	p	r	i	t
o	g	e	l	b	m	e	s	s	a
o	b	o	t	l	b	d	p	e	m
p	r	n	o	o	u	b	l	e	d
r	i	z	z	r	n	t	i	l	p
p	t	b	a	l	d	e	n	o	u
l	t	b	l	e	l	v	o	c	r
e	l	o	e	x	e	n	t	c	p
e	e	t	z	u	p	r	i	i	l
l	w	t	p	z	z	l	t	h	e
c	z	l	n	o	o	d	l	e	t
i	s	e	m	b	l	e	e	v	n
h	s	s	o	t	t	l	b	d	r
e	l	z	z	u	p	u	r	p	p
v	u	n	d	e	l	z	z	v	u

Name _____ Date _____

Consonant + *le* Syllable Speed Drill

1. Underline the consonant + *le* syllable at the end of each word.
2. Pronounce each word with your teacher.
3. Practice reading the words on your own.
4. When you are ready, have a partner time you reading the words for one minute. Keep practicing to improve your speed.

assemble	bible	crumble	durable	fumble	humble	marble	quibble	scramble	thimble
jungle	struggle	wiggle	bundle	handle	noodle	cripple	purple	sprinkle	bicycle
cripple	assemble	sprinkle	quibble	bible	wiggle	purple	fumble	noodle	marble
durable	bundle	humble	handle	jungle	bicycle	crumble	quibble	thimble	scramble
struggle	sprinkle	cripple	assemble	thimble	marble	handle	wiggle	fumble	durable
humble	bible	wiggle	marble	bundle	struggle	scramble	jungle	crumble	purple
sprinkle	noodle	durable	cripple	humble	assemble	noodle	struggle	handle	quibble
thimble	quibble	fumble	scramble	bible	bicycle	crumble	bundle	humble	jungle
bundle	marble	wiggle	thimble	sprinkle	durable	cripple	bible	purple	fumble
crumble	bicycle	scramble	noodle	struggle	purple	assemble	jungle	bicycle	handle

	Words per Minute	Date	Partner
Timed Reading 1	_____	_____	_____
Timed Reading 2	_____	_____	_____
Timed Reading 3	_____	_____	_____

Week-by-Week Phonics & Word Study Activities for the Intermediate Grades • © 2011 by Wiley Blevins • Scholastic Teaching Resources

Name _____ Date _____

High-Frequency Syllable Fluency • Part 1

 Read It

1. Underline the target syllable in each word.
2. Practice reading the words.
3. Cut apart the word cards.
4. See how fast you can sort the words by common syllable.

Syllables 151–160

ern	modern	government	tavern
eve	eve	evening	uneven
hap	happy	happen	hapless
ies	cookies	armies	accessories
ket	market	kettle	basketball
lec	election	**lecture**	collector
main	remain	**domain**	maintenance
mar	marble	marvelous	**margin**
mis	mistake	misery*	misrepresent
my	myself*	**academy**	**economy**

● For Part 2, make a copy of the reproducible on page 159 for each student.

Vowel Team Syllables Mini-lesson

STEP 1

Define

Tell students that sometimes two or more letters together stand for one vowel sound, such as *ai, aw, ay, ea, ee, ew, igh, oa, ow, oo, oi, oy, ou, ie,* and *ei*. These letter pairs are called vowel teams. Since they are a team, they must stay together in the same syllable. This type of syllable is called a **vowel team syllable**. For example, the vowel team syllable in the word *mailbox* is *mail*. (Note: You might need to remind students that in some vowel spellings, consonants such as *y* and *w* act as vowels.)

STEP 2

Transition to Longer Words

Help students transition from reading one-syllable to multisyllabic words. Have them read the simple word in the first column, then use that word to read the multisyllabic word in the second column.

coon	raccoon
teen	canteen
day	holiday
deed	indeed
road	railroad
count	accountant

point	appointment
way	subway
draw	withdraw
pound	compound

STEP 3

Build Words

Write the following word parts on the board:

> *tain, re, enter, con, ceed, ex, pro, right, copy, birth, forth, out, up, ment*

Have student pairs combine the word parts to build as many words as possible. These and other words can be formed:

> *retain, entertain, contain, exceed, proceed, birthright, forthright, outright, upright, entertainment, containment*

STEP 4

Apply Decoding Strategy

Have students use the Decoding Big Words Strategy to decode the following words:

> *complaining, yesterday, bloodstream, seventeen, oversight*

Remind them to look for vowel team syllables in Step 3 of the strategy.

 Teacher-to-Teacher

Creating New Words: A great learning center activity is to list the syllables studied throughout the week. Students list each syllable on paper and then add consonants, blends, digraphs, or word chunks to the syllables to make new words. Challenge students to see how many words they can make.

Name _____ Date _____

Vowel Team Syllables Unscramble It!

1. Unscramble each set of letters to form a word with vowel team syllables.

2. Write the words in the blank.

(1) day   yes   ter   _____

(2) tle   ground   bat   _____

(3) ment   point   ap   _____

(4) day   i   hol   _____

(5) tain   en   ter   _____

(6) ing   plain   com   _____

(7) ing   tain   main   _____

(8) ni   mag   fied   _____

(9) read   proof   ing   _____

(10) dle   nee   point   _____

Name _____ Date _____

Vowel Team Syllable Speed Drill

1. Underline the vowel team (or teams) in each word. Remember that the vowel team must remain in the same syllable.

2. Pronounce each word with your teacher.

3. Practice reading the words on your own.

4. When you are ready, have a partner time you reading the words for one minute. Keep practicing to improve your speed.

maintain	holiday	conceal	succeed	magnified	delight	afloat	disown	proofread	outlawed
default	sirloin	corduroy	pronounce	snowplow	Moscow	curfew	typhoon	likelihood	devoured
pronounce	curfew	default	conceal	sirloin	succeed	snowplow	holiday	typhoon	magnified
proofread	maintain	likelihood	outlawed	corduroy	typhoon	delight	Moscow	holiday	snowplow
curfew	pronounce	delight	disown	succeed	outlawed	magnified	sirloin	snowplow	afloat
delight	default	conceal	devoured	maintain	corduroy	Moscow	afloat	proofread	holiday
typhoon	curfew	devoured	pronounce	disown	Moscow	outlawed	likelihood	maintain	sirloin
magnified	conceal	typhoon	magnified	devoured	succeed	afloat	corduroy	likelihood	proofread
default	likelihood	delight	disown	curfew	pronounce	devoured	proofread	sirloin	outlawed
succeed	disown	Moscow	conceal	default	afloat	snowplow	maintain	corduroy	holiday

	Words per Minute	Date	Partner
Timed Reading 1	_____	_____	_____
Timed Reading 2	_____	_____	_____
Timed Reading 3	_____	_____	_____

Name _____ Date _____

High-Frequency Syllable Fluency • Part 1

Read It

1. Underline the target syllable in each word.
2. Practice reading the words.
3. Cut apart the word cards.
4. See how fast you can sort the words by common syllable.

Syllables 161–170

nal	**journal**	final	**internal**
ness	illness	dizziness	bitterness
ning	running	planning	inning
n't	couldn't	wouldn't	shouldn't
nu	numerous	nutritious	**nuclear**
oc	October	**occupy**	octagon
pres	present	presentation	presidential
sup	supper	supplement	supple
te	**strategic**	**integrate**	tedious
ted	knotted	adopted	educated

● For Part 2, make a copy of the reproducible on page 159 for each student.

Prefixes Mini-lesson *(in-/im-, over-, mis-, sub-)*

STEP 1

Define

Tell students that a **prefix** is a group of letters added to the beginning of a base word to make a new word. The prefix changes the word's meaning. Recognizing common prefixes can help students decode a word and figure out its meaning. For example, the word *unhappy* begins with the prefix *un-*. The prefix *un-* means "not" or "the opposite of." So, someone who is unhappy is <u>not</u> happy. Point out the following prefixes:

- **in-/im-** means "in" or "into"

  The athlete seemed to have an *inborn* ability to swim fast.

  The *immigrants* came to the United States from all over the world.

- **over-** means "too much"

  Please do not *overcook* the meal

- **mis-** means "wrongly" or "bad"

  I must have *misread* your note about when to meet.

- **sub-** means "under"

  We took the *subway* when visiting New York City.

STEP 2

Transition to Longer Words

Help students transition from reading one-syllable to multisyllabic words. Have them read the prefix in the first column, then use that prefix to read and define the multisyllabic word in the second column.

| in | indoors |
| im | immigrant |

over	overact
mis	misplace
sub	subway
in	inborn
im	immerse
over	overtake
mis	misleading
sub	submarine

STEP 3

Build Words

Write the following word parts on the board:

mis, in, im, over, sub, be, have, side, plant, treat, lead, way, group

Have student pairs combine the word parts to build as many words as possible. These and other words can be formed:

misbehave, mistreat, mislead, inside, implant, subway, subgroup

STEP 4

Apply Decoding Strategy

Have students use the Decoding Big Words Strategy to decode the following words:

mispronounced, overshadow, imperil overwhelmingly, subconscious

Remind them to look for prefixes in Step 1 of the strategy.

Name _____ Date _____

Prefixes What's My Word? (*in-/im-, over-, mis-, sub-*)

1. Read each clue.

2. Then look at the incomplete word.

3. Write the missing letters to solve the clue.

1   To cook something too much   ___ ___ ___ ___ c o o k

2   To read a word incorrectly   ___ ___ ___ r e a d

3   An underground train   ___ ___ ___ w a y

4   Not outside   ___ ___ d o o r s

5   I can't find it. I must have _____ it.   ___ ___ ___ p l a c e d

6   A boat under the water   ___ ___ ___ m a r ___ n ___

7   To treat badly   ___ ___ s ___ r e ___ ___

8   To bring goods into a country   ___ ___ p ___ r t

9   To get too hot   ___ ___ ___ ___ h ___ ___ t

10   A person who moves from one country to another   ___ ___ m i g ___ ___ n t

Name _____ Date _____

Prefix Speed Drill (in-/im-, over-, mis-, sub-)

1. Underline the prefix that begins each word.
2. Pronounce each word with your teacher.
3. Practice reading the words on your own.
4. When you are ready, have a partner time you reading the words for one minute. Keep practicing to improve your speed.

indoors	import	overheat	misname	subway	infested	mislocate	overcast	misread	subgroup
immerse	overcrowded	overrate	misjudge	submarine	implant	subconscious	oversized	misguided	submerge
import	subway	subconscious	overheat	indoors	submarine	infested	misname	implant	mislocate
misjudge	immerse	import	overcrowded	subway	overcast	implant	mislocate	misread	overheat
infested	misjudge	overcrowded	immerse	implant	misname	overrate	indoors	oversized	submarine
subconscious	subgroup	submerge	import	overcast	immerse	oversized	misread	subgroup	subway
overcrowded	infested	mislocate	implant	submerge	misread	overheat	submerge	indoors	overrate
subway	subconscious	misname	misjudge	immerse	overheat	overcast	subgroup	submarine	misguided
misguided	misname	overrate	misread	infested	oversized	subconscious	overcrowded	misguided	indoors
mislocate	submerge	misjudge	oversized	import	subgroup	misguided	overcast	overrate	submarine

	Words per Minute	Date	Partner
Timed Reading 1	_____	_____	_____
Timed Reading 2	_____	_____	_____
Timed Reading 3	_____	_____	_____

Name _____ Date _____

High-Frequency Syllable Fluency • Part 1

 Read It

1. Underline the target syllable in each word.
2. Practice reading the words.
3. Cut apart the word cards.
4. See how fast you can sort the words by common syllable.

Syllables 171–180

tem	**item**	temper	**temporary**
tin	tinfoil	tinsel	continue
tri	triangle	triumph	**contribute***
tro	astronaut	Trojan War	**controversy**
up	uphill	update	upheaval
va	vacation	vapor	vacant
ven	venom	vendor	ventilate
vis	visitor	revisit	**vision***
am	ambulance	amateur	amphibian
bor	boring	border	neighbor

● For Part 2, make a copy of the reproducible on page 159 for each student.

Review and Assess

Assessment Directions

1. Make one copy of the Real Word Test (page 94) and the Nonsense Word Test (page 95). You may wish to make the copy on cardstock for greater durability.

2. Make one copy of the Assessment Scoring Sheet (page 93) for each student.

3. Assess students individually. Have each student read the words from the Real Word Test, then the Nonsense Word Test.

4. Place a checkmark (✓) in the second column for each word read correctly. If the student correctly reads the word but does so in a slow, labored manner, place a check minus (✓–) in the second column to indicate that fluency (automaticity with the sound-spellings) may still be an issue.

5. If the student incorrectly reads the word, record his or her attempt. Analyze the errors to notice patterns of difficulty. For example, some students might be overrelying on the initial letters in a word and not fully analyzing it. Other students might have difficulties with one specific aspect of the word, such as a complex spelling pattern. This analysis will inform the next steps you take to address these issues. During small-group instructional time, continue working with students on those skills not mastered.

6. Tally the scores from both tests. Students should be able to read the words with a minimum of 80% accuracy (i.e., 24 correct out of 30).

7. Create an Action Plan for students who struggle with specific skills (accuracy or speed issues) or students who fall below the 80% level. These students will need additional instruction, practice, and review on the skills covered in the lessons.

Assessment Scoring Sheet

Place a checkmark (✓) in the second column if the student reads the word correctly. If the student correctly reads the word but does so in a slow, labored manner, place a check minus (✓–) in the second column. If the student reads the word incorrectly, record the student's attempt.

Student Name: _____

Date: _____

Real Word Test	
1. maple	
2. squiggle	
3. replay	
4. mistreated	
5. disappear	
6. nonfiction	
7. definition	
8. visitor	
9. brightly	
10. gardener	
11. biology	
12. photograph	
13. microscope	
14. thermometer	
15. description	
16. inspector	
17. construction	
18. distract	
19. overtake	
20. subgroup	

Nonsense Word Test	
1. fubble	
2. squizzled	
3. reatloid	
4. flayveen	
5. disgroam	
6. nonsleft	
7. photobleck	
8. camtion	
9. overspesh	
10. thermopask	

Scores: _____ Real Word Test

_____ Nonsense Word Test

_____ Total Score

Fluency: ❑ Good

❑ Poor

Skills Needing Additional Work:

Action Plan:

Name _____ Date _____

Real Word Test

1. maple	11. biology
2. squiggle	12. photograph
3. replay	13. microscope
4. mistreated	14. thermometer
5. disappear	15. description
6. nonfiction	16. inspector
7. definition	17. construction
8. visitor	18. distract
9. brightly	19. overtake
10. gardener	20. subgroup

Name _____ Date _____

Nonsense Word Test

1. fubble

2. squizzled

3. reatloid

4. flayveen

5. disgroam

6. nonsleft

7. photobleck

8. camtion

9. overspesh

10. thermopask

r-Controlled Vowel Syllables Mini-lesson

STEP 1

Define

Tell students that when a vowel is followed by the letter *r*, it usually affects the vowel sound, as in *ar*, *er*, *ir*, *or*, and *ur*. The vowel and the letter *r* act as a team. Therefore, they must remain in the same syllable. This is called an **r-controlled vowel syllable**. For example, the *r*-controlled vowel syllable in the word *market* is *mar*.

STEP 2

Transition to Longer Words

Help students transition from reading one-syllable to multisyllabic words. Have them read the *r*-controlled vowel syllable in the first column, then use that syllable to read the multisyllabic word in the second column.

mar	marble
car	carton
gar	garlic
per	perfect
ner	dinner
cir	circus
for	forty

mor	rumor
bur	burden
urb	suburb

STEP 3

Build Words

Write the following word parts on the board:

> dis, re, land, ob, for, gar, gard, mark, turb,
> serve, ty, lic, mal, nish, den

Have student pairs combine the word parts to build as many words as possible. These and other words can be formed:

> disregard, disturb, regard, reserve,
> remark, landmark, observe, forty,
> formal, garlic, garnish, garden

STEP 4

Apply Decoding Strategy

Have students use the Decoding Big Words Strategy to decode the following words:

> merchandise, flirtatious, distortion,
> duration, endurance

Remind them to look for *r*-controlled vowel syllables in Step 3 of the strategy.

 Teacher-to-Teacher

Building Vocabulary: Write words from the week on index cards. Play Password using the cards. A student draws a card, then provides clues for the rest of the class to figure out the word; for example: "My word has two syllables. The first syllable is a sound a cat makes. My word means 'flawless or great.' What's my word?" (perfect) This is a great vocabulary-building game.

Name _____ Date _____

r-Controlled Vowel Syllables What's My Word?

1. Read each clue.
2. Look at the incomplete word.
3. Write the missing letters to solve the clue.

(1) Person who draws or paints ___ ___ t i s t

(2) Person who cuts hair b ___ ___ b ___ ___

(3) Place with clowns and trapezes ___ ___ ___ c u s

(4) Where you plant vegetables g ___ ___ d ___ n

(5) Who you see when you are ill ___ ___ c t ___ ___

(6) The meal after lunch ___ i n ___ ___ ___

(7) Opposite of exit ___ n ___ ___ ___

(8) A scary creature m ___ ___ s ___ ___ ___

(9) Opposite of rural ___ ___ b a n

(10) A number halfway between 30 and 50 ___ ___ ___ t y

Write your own clues below for a classmate to answer.

(11) _____ ___ ___ ___ ___

(12) _____ ___ ___ ___ ___

Name _____ Date _____

r-Controlled Vowel Syllable Speed Drill

1. Underline the *r*-controlled vowel syllable in each word.
2. Pronounce each word with your teacher.
3. Practice reading the words on your own.
4. When you are ready, have a partner time you reading the words for one minute. Keep practicing to improve your speed.

urgent	torture	vertical	pardon	thirsty	skirmish	slender	nurture	harvest	merchant
fortress	curtain	certify	blister	afford	burden	carbon	formal	hunger	perfectly
torture	harvest	perfectly	vertical	urgent	blister	thirsty	perfectly	skirmish	pardon
afford	formal	fortress	certify	curtain	nurture	merchant	thirsty	burden	blister
certify	torture	vertical	urgent	merchant	certify	pardon	carbon	torture	slender
slender	perfectly	nurture	formal	skirmish	curtain	fortress	burden	harvest	perfectly
hunger	afford	skirmish	carbon	formal	pardon	harvest	fortress	thirsty	carbon
certify	urgent	hunger	vertical	afford	nurture	burden	slender	hunger	torture
pardon	hunger	merchant	skirmish	merchant	slender	curtain	formal	blister	fortress
urgent	carbon	vertical	blister	burden	harvest	afford	nurture	curtain	thirsty

	Words per Minute	Date	Partner
Timed Reading 1	_____	_____	_____
Timed Reading 2	_____	_____	_____
Timed Reading 3	_____	_____	_____

Name _____ Date _____

High-Frequency Syllable Fluency • Part 1

Read It

1. Underline the target syllable in each word.
2. Practice reading the words.
3. Cut apart the word cards.
4. See how fast you can sort the words by common syllable.

Syllables 181–190

by	bypass	bystanders	whereby
cat	cattle	catalog	**category**
cent	percent	accent	**adjacent**
ev	every	evolution	**evident**
gan	began	gigantic	gander
gle	eagle	angle	gurgle
head	headache	headphones	arrowhead
high	highway	higher education	highbrow
il	illegal	**illustrate**	illiterate
lu	lunar	**revolution**	lucrative

● For Part 2, make a copy of the reproducible on page 159 for each student.

Final e Syllables Mini-lesson

STEP 1

Define

Tell students that the spellings *a_e*, *e_e*, *i_e*, *o_e*, and *u_e* often stand for long vowel sounds as in *cake*, *eve*, *like*, *bone*, and *cute*. We call these vowel spellings final *e*, or silent *e*, spellings. These vowel spellings are unique because the two letters forming the vowel sound do not appear side by side in the word. However, they still act as a team and cannot be separated. Therefore, they must remain in the same syllable. We call this syllable the **final e syllable**. For example, the final e syllable in the word *delete* is *lete*.

STEP 2

Transition to Longer Words

Help students transition from reading one-syllable to multisyllabic words. Have them read the simple word or syllable in the first column, then use that word or syllable to read the multisyllabic word in the second column.

side	inside
vade	invade
fine	refine
made	unmade
plete	complete
hope	hopeless

side	sideways
shame	shameful
wide	widespread
lone	lonely

STEP 3

Build Words

Write the following word parts on the board:

> *in, a, com, side, vite, sane, lone, muse, maze, pare, pete, plete, bine*

Have student pairs combine the word parts to build as many words as possible. These and other words can be formed:

> *inside, invite, insane, alone, amuse, amaze, compare, compete, complete, combine*

STEP 4

Apply Decoding Strategy

Have students use the Decoding Big Words Strategy to decode the following words:

> *captivate, membrane, stampede, xylophone, extremely*

Remind them to look for final *e* syllables in Step 3 of the strategy.

 **Teacher-to-Teacher**

Exceptions to the Long Vowel Sound: There are some high-frequency words with final *e* spellings that do not form long vowel sounds. These include *come, some, love, have, one, done, give, live, once, were*. Students should be aware of these exceptions.

Name _____ Date _____

Final e Syllables Word Search

 Find It

1. Find and circle the following words.
2. The words can be across, up and down, or on the diagonal. Some are written backwards.

advice   athlete   combine   erase   feline   female   incomplete   inside   invade   severe

p	i	f	e	q	d	m	n	x	i
c	n	e	h	w	f	k	l	f	n
o	s	l	e	n	i	l	e	f	w
m	c	o	m	v	t	m	g	h	e
b	f	f	e	h	a	h	y	r	a
i	e	t	e	l	h	t	a	i	s
n	t	r	e	m	n	l	n	n	e
e	r	a	a	e	v	e	f	l	i
e	e	i	a	s	w	g	e	e	n
a	d	v	i	c	e	f	r	r	s
d	a	s	b	n	m	d	e	e	i
s	v	m	o	c	e	v	v	f	d
i	n	c	o	m	p	l	e	t	e
x	i	y	u	i	o	p	s	d	s
w	g	j	c	o	a	t	h	l	d

Name _____ Date _____

Final *e* Syllable Speed Drill

1. Underline the final *e* syllable in each word.
2. Pronounce each word with your teacher.
3. Practice reading the words on your own.
4. When you are ready, have a partner time you reading the words for one minute. Keep practicing to improve your speed.

abuse	athlete	collide	delete	erase	female	ignite	inside	translate	severe
advice	blockade	combine	donate	escape	feline	insane	notebook	provide	hopeless
athlete	translate	feline	advice	collide	blockade	erase	donate	inside	ignite
ignite	female	abuse	combine	advice	escape	delete	severe	notebook	inside
feline	combine	insane	athlete	notebook	severe	abuse	advice	donate	erase
translate	ignite	female	provide	insane	notebook	blockade	collide	female	delete
combine	feline	translate	severe	delete	donate	erase	athlete	escape	advice
severe	donate	erase	hopeless	collide	provide	insane	inside	blockade	abuse
insane	provide	delete	combine	translate	ignite	hopeless	escape	notebook	inside
hopeless	athlete	provide	abuse	feline	escape	collide	blockade	hopeless	female

	Words per Minute	Date	Partner
Timed Reading 1	_____	_____	_____
Timed Reading 2	_____	_____	_____
Timed Reading 3	_____	_____	_____

Name _____ Date _____

High-Frequency Syllable Fluency • Part 1

 Read It

1. Underline the target syllable in each word.
2. Practice reading the words.
3. Cut apart the word cards.
4. See how fast you can sort the words by common syllable.

Syllables 191–200

me	meteor	**media**	**intermediate**
nor	normal	ignoring	governor
part	apart	**partner**	department
por	**portion**	important	portal
read	misread*	ready	readily
rep	represent	repetition	replica
su	super	superbly	supersonic
tend	attend	intend	pretended
ther	other	brotherly	**furthermore**
ton	carton	cotton	skeleton

● For Part 2, make a copy of the reproducible on page 159 for each student.

Prefixes Mini-lesson (*pre-, inter-, fore-, de-*)

STEP 1

Define

Tell students that a **prefix** is a group of letters added to the beginning of a base word to make a new word. The prefix changes the word's meaning. Recognizing common prefixes can help students decode a word and figure out its meaning. For example, the word *unhappy* begins with the prefix *un-*. The prefix *un-* means "not" or "the opposite of." So, someone who is unhappy is <u>not</u> happy. Point out the following prefixes:

- **pre-** means "before"

  The letter *a precedes* the letter *r* in the word *car*.

- **inter-** means "between" or "among"

  We drove on the *interstate* highway for ten hours.

- **fore-** means "before" or "ahead of time" or "the front of"

  The weather reporter *forecasted* this terrible storm.

  I burned my *forearm* in the accident.

- **de-** means "opposite of" or "undo" or "take away/remove"

  Can you *decode* the secret message?

  Mom needed to *defrost* the chicken before cooking dinner.

STEP 2

Transition to Longer Words

Help students transition from reading one-syllable to multisyllabic words. Have them read the word in the first column, then add a prefix to that word to read and define the multisyllabic word in the second column.

war	prewar
state	interstate
thought	forethought
code	decode
season	preseason
mix	intermix
word	foreword
frost	defrost

STEP 3

Build Words

Write the following word parts on the board:

> *pre, inter, fore, de, cut, game, plan, act, lock, cast, go, ground, plane, rail, throne*

Have student pairs combine the word parts to build as many words as possible. These and other words can be formed:

> *precut, pregame, preplan, interact, interlock, forecast, forego, foreground, deplane, derail, dethrone*

STEP 4

Apply Decoding Strategy

Have students use the Decoding Big Words Strategy to decode the following words:

> *prearrange, prequalify, international, forethought, decompose*

Remind them to look for prefixes in Step 1 of the strategy.

Name _____ Date _____

Prefixes Prefix or Pretender? (*pre-, inter-, fore-, de-*)

1. Read each word pair.
2. Put an X over the word in each pair that does NOT begin with a prefix. Remember, after the prefix is removed, a base word must remain.

(1) presents   preheat

(2) interstate   interesting

(3) declawed   decorate

(4) interior   interactions

(5) preschool   precious

(6) deposit   deface

(7) forensic   forethought

(8) decisions   deflate

(9) preordered   presentation

(10) forecaster   foreign

(11) international   internal

(12) forest   foreground

Write sentences using one or more of the prefixed words above.

(13) _____

_____

_____

(14) _____

_____

_____

(15) _____

_____

_____

Name _____ Date _____

Prefix Speed Drill *(pre-, inter-, fore-, de-)*

1. Underline the prefix that begins each word.
2. Pronounce each word with your teacher.
3. Practice reading the words on your own.
4. When you are ready, have a partner time you reading the words for one minute. Keep practicing to improve your speed.

preheat	interact	forecast	debug	prejudge	international	forehead	declaw	preplan	intermix
foreshadow	deflate	preorder	intersect	foretell	deplane	prewash	interstate	forewarn	decompose
forecast	prejudge	interact	interstate	preheat	foretell	declaw	deplane	international	forehead
preorder	foreshadow	forecast	deflate	prejudge	prewash	debug	intermix	decompose	deplane
preplan	intersect	preorder	interact	deflate	international	preheat	foretell	forehead	declaw
interstate	preplan	foreshadow	decompose	forecast	deflate	prejudge	forewarn	foretell	debug
intersect	interstate	international	prewash	interact	intermix	forehead	deflate	preheat	decompose
international	intersect	intermix	debug	preorder	declaw	deplane	prejudge	forewarn	forecast
decompose	intermix	declaw	prewash	forehead	forewarn	interact	foreshadow	preplan	forewarn
preheat	prewash	debug	foreshadow	preplan	deplane	preorder	interstate	intersect	foretell

	Words per Minute	Date	Partner
Timed Reading 1	_____	_____	_____
Timed Reading 2	_____	_____	_____
Timed Reading 3	_____	_____	_____

Name _____ Date _____

High-Frequency Syllable Fluency • Part 1

 Read It

1. Underline the target syllable in each word.
2. Practice reading the words.
3. Cut apart the word cards.
4. See how fast you can sort the words by common syllable.

Syllables 201–210

try	entry	country	poultry
um	umpire	umbrella	**medium**
uer	rescuer*	leaguer	cataloguer
way	highway	driveway	wayward
ate	**appropriate**	**accurate**	**corporate**
bet	better	alphabet	diabetic
bles	marbles	crumbles	foibles
bod	body	busybody	antibodies
cap	capital	capsule	capture
cial	special	artificial	**crucial**

● For Part 2, make a copy of the reproducible on page 159 for each student.

Suffixes Mini-lesson (-ible/-able, -al/-ial, -y, -ness)

STEP 1

Define

Tell students that a **suffix** is a letter or group of letters added to the end of a base word. A suffix changes the word's meaning and often its part of speech. For example, the suffix -ed is added to the word *depart* (*departed*) to indicate that the action happened in the past. Point out the following suffixes:

- **-ible/-able** used to mean "can be done" or "capable of" (digestible, breakable), "likely to" (agreeable), and "worthy of" (lovable) (This suffix turns the root word into an adjective.)

  Many believed the Titanic was *unsinkable*.

  That was the most *horrible* movie I have ever seen.

- **-al/-ial** used to show "having characteristics of"

  We collected *historical* facts and documents for the report.

- **-y** used to show "characterized by"

  It was a warm and *breezy* day.

- **-ness** used to show "state of" or "condition of" (This suffix forms a noun.)

  Her *happiness* at the good news spread to all of us.

STEP 2

Transition to Longer Words

Help students transition from reading one-syllable to multisyllabic words. Have them read the suffix in the first column, then use that suffix to read the multisyllabic word in the second column.

able	laughable
ible	invisible
al	historical
y	gloomy
ness	politeness
able	predictable
ible	legible
ial	crucial
y	rubbery
ness	goodness

STEP 3

Build Words

Write the following word parts on the board:

ness, y, able, al, dark, sad, weak, accept, break, enjoy, accident, comic, education, meat, tooth, pick

Have student pairs combine the word parts to build as many words as possible. These and other words can be formed:

darkness, sadness, weakness, acceptable, breakable, enjoyable, accidental, comical, educational, meaty, toothy, picky

STEP 4

Apply Decoding Strategy

Have students use the Decoding Big Words Strategy to decode the following words:

unhappiness, spidery, conventional, technological, unforgettable

Remind them to look for suffixes in Step 2 of the strategy.

Name _____ Date _____

Suffixes B-I-N-G-O (-ible/-able, -al/-ial, -y, -ness)

1. Write one of the following words randomly in each blank on the B-I-N-G-O board:

   accidental, agreeable, artificial, crucial, essential, happiness, historical, illnesses, invisible, laughable, politeness, valuable, gloomy

   You may use a word more than once.

2. Mark each word on the board as your teacher calls it.

B	I	N	G	O
		FREE		

Name _____ Date _____

Suffix Speed Drill (-ible/-able, -al/-ial, -y, -ness)

1. Underline the suffix that ends each word.
2. Pronounce each word with your teacher.
3. Practice reading the words on your own.
4. When you are ready, have a partner time you reading the words for one minute.
   Keep practicing to improve your speed.

accidental	hefty	lovable	darkness	artificial	sweaty	valuable	happiness	essential	liquidy
illegible	weakness	historical	itchy	inedible	illness	political	catchy	visible	greatness
artificial	essential	hefty	illegible	itchy	lovable	catchy	weakness	valuable	political
essential	darkness	illegible	visible	sweaty	accidental	happiness	political	liquidy	illness
illegible	historical	inedible	hefty	visible	valuable	political	lovable	catchy	happiness
valuable	artificial	accidental	darkness	itchy	sweaty	illness	liquidy	weakness	catchy
inedible	essential	visible	political	greatness	hefty	liquidy	sweaty	greatness	weakness
historical	happiness	artificial	lovable	inedible	greatness	darkness	itchy	illness	hefty
itchy	lovable	historical	essential	happiness	inedible	weakness	greatness	accidental	sweaty
accidental	artificial	valuable	illegible	visible	liquidy	illness	historical	catchy	darkness

	Words per Minute	Date	Partner
Timed Reading 1	_____	_____	_____
Timed Reading 2	_____	_____	_____
Timed Reading 3	_____	_____	_____

Week-by-Week Phonics & Word Study Activities for the Intermediate Grades • © 2011 by Wiley Blevins • Scholastic Teaching Resources

Name _____ Date _____

High-Frequency Syllable Fluency • Part 1

 Read It

1. Underline the target syllable in each word.
2. Practice reading the words.
3. Cut apart the word cards.
4. See how fast you can sort the words by common syllable.

Syllables 211–220

cir	circle	circus	**circumstance**
cor	corner	**correspond**	**incorporate**
coun	council	counselor	counterfeit
cus	custom	**focus**	custodian
dan	dandruff	bandanna	dandelion
dle	cradle	saddle	bundle
ef	effort	effect	efficient
end	endless	bookend	unending
ent	different	excellent	**apparent**
ered	flowered	airpowered	empowered

● For Part 2, make a copy of the reproducible on page 159 for each student.

Greek Roots Mini-lesson (number roots)

STEP 1

Define

Tell students that a **root** is a basic word part that gives a word the most important part of its meaning. Many English words have roots from Greek, the language of the people from ancient Greece. Sometimes Greek roots are combined to form larger words. For example, the Greek roots *auto* and *graph* are used to form the word *autograph*. Teach the meanings of the following Greek roots and combining forms:

- **hemi** means "half" (hemisphere)
- **mono** means "one" (monorail)
- **tri** means "three" (tricycle, triplets, triangle)
- **pent** means "five" (Pentagon, the five-sided government building)
- **hex** means "six" (hexagon, like a STOP sign)
- **oct** means "eight" (octagon)
- **deca** means "ten" (decade = ten years)

STEP 2

Transition to Longer Words

Help students transition from reading one-syllable to multisyllabic words. Have them read the Greek root in the first column, then use that root to read the multisyllabic word in the second column. Help students use the root to determine the meaning of the word.

| hemi | hemisphere |
| mono | monorail |

 Teacher-to-Teacher

tri	tricycle
tri	trilogy
pent	pentagon
hex	hexagon
oct	octopus
deca	decade

STEP 3

Build Words

Write the following word parts on the board:

mon, mono, tri, arch, poly, k, graph, rail, tone, logy, sect, cycle, llion, o, ple

Have student pairs combine the word parts to build as many words as possible. These and other words can be formed:

monarch, monopoly, monk, monograph, monorail, monotone, trilogy, trisect, tricycle, trillion, trio, triple

STEP 4

Apply Decoding Strategy

Have students use the Decoding Big Words Strategy to decode the following words:

trisection, monopolize, monastery, octagonal, tricentennial

Remind them to look for Greek roots in Step 3 of the strategy.

Using Roots to Determine Meaning: Discuss how to use roots to determine word meaning; for example, a *triangle* has "three" sides, a *trident* has "three" points, a *tricycle* has "three" wheels, and a *trilogy* is a book series with "three" books in it.

Name _____ Date _____

Greek Roots Word Web (number roots)

1. Work with a partner.

2. Write all the words with the Greek root *tri-* you know in the web.

3. Search a dictionary for more *tri-* words.

4. Write a brief definition of each word to help you remember it.

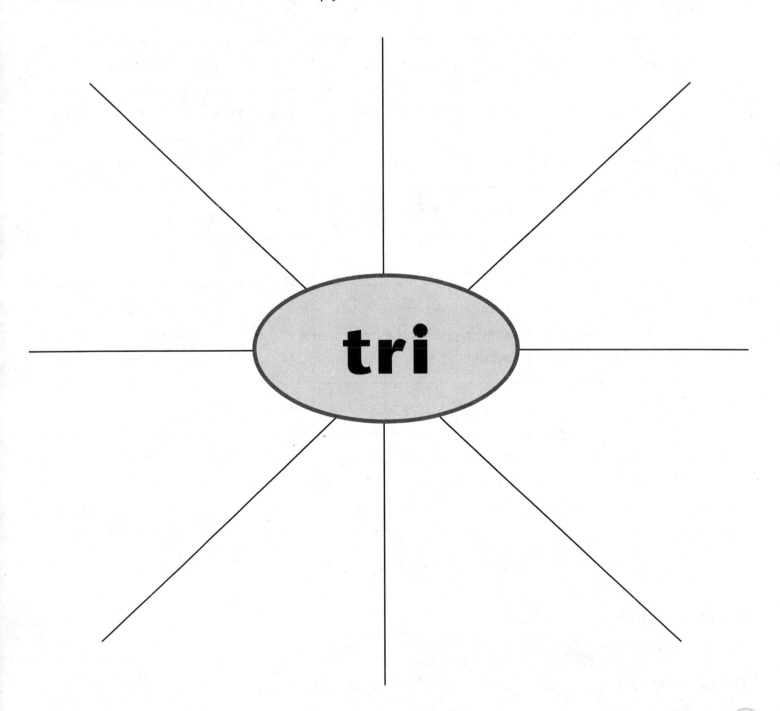

Name _____ Date _____

Greek Root Speed Drill (number roots)

1. Underline the Greek root in each word.

2. Pronounce each word with your teacher.

3. Practice reading the words on your own.

4. When you are ready, have a partner time you reading the words for one minute.
Keep practicing to improve your speed.

monarch	tricycle	monologue	trio	triplet	decathlon	monk	triple	monorail	decade
trident	monotone	trilogy	pentagon	trisect	octagon	octopus	hemisphere	monopoly	hexagon
decathlon	tricycle	monopoly	monotone	pentagon	decade	octagon	triple	trisect	monk
trio	monarch	monorail	decade	tricycle	octagon	monk	hemisphere	monologue	triplet
trilogy	octopus	hemisphere	trident	hexagon	monotone	trilogy	pentagon	hexagon	hemisphere
monorail	trio	decathlon	octagon	monarch	monopoly	monologue	triple	triplet	trisect
octopus	hemisphere	trident	decade	monk	triple	trio	monotone	trident	trilogy
decade	tricycle	monk	hexagon	monologue	decathlon	triplet	pentagon	hexagon	monarch
monopoly	octagon	monologue	monopoly	monorail	pentagon	octopus	trilogy	trisect	trident
tricycle	octopus	triplet	triple	trisect	monarch	monotone	monorail	trio	decathlon

	Words per Minute	Date	Partner
Timed Reading 1	_____	_____	_____
Timed Reading 2	_____	_____	_____
Timed Reading 3	_____	_____	_____

Name _____ Date _____

High-Frequency Syllable Fluency • Part 1

Read It

1. Underline the target syllable in each word.

2. Practice reading the words.

3. Cut apart the word cards.

4. See how fast you can sort the words by common syllable.

Syllables 221–230

fin	finish	Finland	finicky
form	perform	**conform**	**transform**
go	going	gopher	**undergo**
har	harvest	harness	harmony
ish	childish	bluish	outlandish
lands	islands	wetlands	highlands
let	letter	lettuce	inlet
long	belong	longest	longings
mat	matter	mattress	**format**
meas	measure	measurement	measurable

● For Part 2, make a copy of the reproducible on page 159 for each student.

Latin Roots Mini-lesson (number roots)

STEP 1

Define

Tell students that a **root** is a basic word part that gives a word the most important part of its meaning. Many English words have roots from Latin, the language of the ancient Romans. For example, the Latin root *port* is used to form the word *portable*. The root *port* means "carried" or "moved." Something that is *portable* is easily moved from place to place. Teach the meanings of the following Latin roots:

- **semi** means "half" (semisweet, semicircle)
- **uni** means "one" (uniform, unicycle, unite)
- **du, duo, bi** mean "two" (duplicate, double, bilingual, bicycle)
- **quad/quart** mean "four" (quadrangle, quadruple, quarter)
- **centi** means "hundred" (centipede, centimeter, bicentennial)
- **milli** means "thousand" (million, millipede)

STEP 2

Transition to Longer Words

Help students transition from reading one-syllable to multisyllabic words. Have them read the Latin root in the first column, then use that root to read the multisyllabic word in the second column. Help students use the root to determine the meaning of the word.

semi	semicircle	semi	semifinal
uni	unicorn	uni	uniform
bi	biweekly	du	duplicate
quad	quadruple	quart	quarter
centi	centimeter	milli	millionaire

STEP 3

Build Words

Write the following word parts on the board:

uni, bi, cent, corn, form, fy, que, on, versity, sect, ceps, llion, month, ly, per, ury, meter, i, grade

Have student pairs combine the word parts to build as many words as possible. These and other words can be formed:

unicorn, uniform, unify, unique, union, university, bisect, billion, bimonthly, percent, century, centimeter, centigrade

STEP 4

Apply Decoding Strategy

Have students use the Decoding Big Words Strategy to decode the following words:

semicolon, unanimously, bicentennial, quadruplet, centipede

Remind them to look for Latin roots in Step 3 of the strategy.

 Teacher-to-Teacher

Using Roots to Determine Meaning: Discuss how to use roots to determine word meaning. For example, a *uniform* is "one" outfit that all the people at a place wear; *unison* is when people act as "one" when speaking or singing; *unify* means to bring together as "one"; and a *union* is a group of workers acting as "one."

Name _____ Date _____

Latin Roots Word Web (number roots)

1. Work with a partner.
2. Write all the words with the Latin root *uni-* you know in the web.
3. Search a dictionary for more *uni-* words.
4. Add a brief definition of each word to help you remember it.
5. On another sheet of paper, create a word web for the Latin root *bi-* or *cent-*.

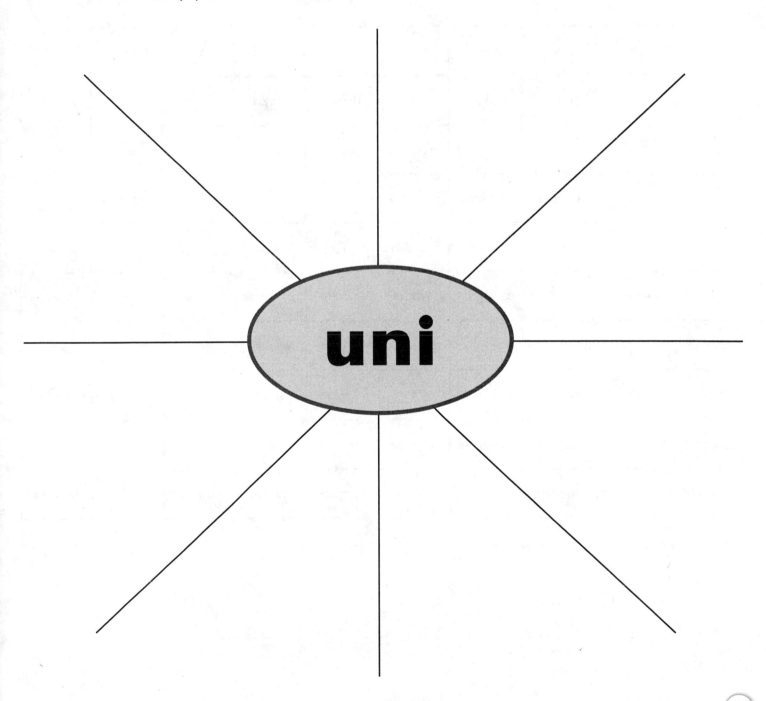

Name _____ Date _____

Latin Root Speed Drill

1. Underline the Latin number root in each word.
2. Pronounce each word with your teacher.
3. Practice reading the words on your own.
4. When you are ready, have a partner time you reading the words for one minute.
   Keep practicing to improve your speed.

biweekly	uniform	duplicate	bicycle	unanimous	quarter	semicircle	century	centipede	million
quadruple	biracial	square	biannual	bisect	duplex	unicycle	unite	percent	unicorn
unanimous	percent	biweekly	duplicate	biannual	square	bicycle	centipede	century	million
unite	quadruple	biracial	uniform	centipede	unicycle	quarter	bicycle	semicircle	biannual
bisect	unanimous	duplex	biracial	biweekly	duplicate	square	million	quarter	century
million	unicycle	quadruple	centipede	biracial	uniform	semicircle	unite	bicycle	square
biannual	bisect	unanimous	unicycle	semicircle	percent	biweekly	unicorn	square	quarter
duplex	semicircle	million	quadruple	century	duplicate	percent	uniform	unicorn	bicycle
centipede	century	duplex	unanimous	unicycle	bisect	biannual	unite	biweekly	duplicate
percent	unite	unicorn	bisect	duplex	quadruple	unicorn	quarter	biracial	uniform

	Words per Minute	Date	Partner
Timed Reading 1	_____	_____	_____
Timed Reading 2	_____	_____	_____
Timed Reading 3	_____	_____	_____

Name _____ Date _____

High-Frequency Syllable Fluency • Part 1

 Read It

1. Underline the target syllable in each word.
2. Practice reading the words.
3. Cut apart the word cards.
4. See how fast you can sort the words by common syllable.

Syllables 231–240

mem	member	membrane	remembrance
mul	multiple	multitude	multinational
ner	nervous	beginner	partnership
play	playful	playground	displaying
ples	apples	couples	**principles**
ply	reply	multiply	**imply**
port	report	**transport**	import
press	pressing	**depress**	expression*
sat	Saturday	Saturn	satellite
sec	second	**section**	**sector**

● For Part 2, make a copy of the reproducible on page 159 for each student.

r-Controlled Vowel Syllables Mini-lesson

 STEP 1

Define

Tell students that when a vowel is followed by the letter *r*, it usually affects the vowel sound, as in *ar*, *er*, *ir*, *or*, and *ur*. The vowel and the letter *r* act as a team. Therefore, they must remain in the same syllable. This is called an **r-controlled vowel syllable**. For example, the *r*-controlled vowel syllable in the word *market* is *mar*.

STEP 2

Transition to Longer Words

Help students transition from reading one-syllable to multisyllabic words. Have them read the *r*-controlled vowel syllable in the first column, then use that syllable to read the multisyllabic word in the second column.

jar	jargon
her	hermit
ger	hunger
ter	blister
por	vapor
cert	concert
dir	dirtiest
ur	urgently
tur	turkey
nor	normally

 STEP 3

Build Words

Write the following word parts on the board in random order:

> *un, re, pre, ed, ing, birth, turn, concern, serve, der, fer, born*

Have student pairs use the word parts to build as many words as possible. These and other words can be formed:

> *unconcerned, unborn, rebirth, return, returned, returning, prebirth, preserve, under, prefer*

 STEP 4

Apply Decoding Strategy

Have students use the Decoding Big Words Strategy to decode the following words:

> *contortionist, forevermore, seminar, nocturnal, reservations*

Remind them to look for *r*-controlled vowel syllables in Step 3 of the strategy.

 Teacher-to-Teacher

Missing Words: Write a brief story or paragraph on chart paper. Place a self-sticking note over every tenth (or so) word. Have students determine which word is covered up. Provide meaning clues or write one syllable at a time until students determine the missing word.

Name _____ Date _____

r-Controlled Vowel Syllables Crossword Puzzle

1. Read the puzzle clues.

2. To answer each clue, select from the words in the box.

3. Write the correct word in the puzzle.

arson
garlic
hermit
nocturnal
razor
remark
turkey
urban
urgent
vapor

Across

3. thin, watery mist

5. to say

6. strong-smelling plant related to an onion

10. popular Thanksgiving food

Down

1. used to cut a beard

2. happening at night

4. needing to be done very quickly

7. illegally setting a fire

8. city living

9. someone who lives alone and away from all people

Name _____ Date _____

r-Controlled Vowel Syllable Speed Drill

1. Underline the *r*-controlled vowel syllable in each word.
2. Pronounce each word with your teacher.
3. Practice reading the words on your own.
4. When you are ready, have a partner time you reading the words for one minute. Keep practicing to improve your speed.

vaporize	turkey	urban	stardom	servant	razor	rebirth	absorb	arson	cancerous
concert	distortion	expert	garlic	hermit	jargon	lunar	immortal	virtue	dirty
urban	immortal	concert	lunar	garlic	turkey	jargon	expert	servant	arson
arson	expert	vaporize	hermit	stardom	garlic	absorb	rebirth	cancerous	dirty
stardom	hermit	distortion	absorb	immortal	concert	servant	turkey	jargon	razor
lunar	urban	rebirth	immortal	vaporize	virtue	distortion	razor	virtue	expert
absorb	arson	lunar	servant	virtue	stardom	dirty	concert	turkey	rebirth
hermit	dirty	urban	garlic	expert	vaporize	razor	cancerous	distortion	concert
distortion	servant	hermit	absorb	razor	lunar	cancerous	jargon	vaporize	stardom
immortal	rebirth	garlic	urban	cancerous	arson	jargon	virtue	dirty	turkey

	Words per Minute	Date	Partner
Timed Reading 1	_____	_____	_____
Timed Reading 2	_____	_____	_____
Timed Reading 3	_____	_____	_____

Name _____ Date _____

High-Frequency Syllable Fluency • Part 1

 Read It

1. Underline the target syllable in each word.
2. Practice reading the words.
3. Cut apart the word cards.
4. See how fast you can sort the words by common syllable.

Syllables 241–250

ser	servant	service	eraser
south	Southwest	Southeast	southern*
sun	sunshine	sunset	sundae
the	**nonetheless**	**nevertheless**	**theory***
ting	fitting	babysitting	earsplitting
tra	**tradition**	**contradict**	trapeze*
tures	**cultures**	**features**	**infrastructures**
val	valley	**valid**	**evaluate**
var	**vary**	various	variation
vid	video	David	individually

● For Part 2, make a copy of the reproducible on page 159 for each student.

Final *e* Syllables Mini-lesson

STEP 1

Define

Tell students that the spellings *a_e*, *e_e*, *i_e*, *o_e*, and *u_e* often stand for long vowel sounds as in *cake*, *eve*, *like*, *bone*, and *cute*. We call these vowel spellings final *e*, or silent *e*, spellings. These vowel spellings are unique because the two letters forming the vowel sound do not appear side by side in the word. However, they still act as a team and cannot be separated. Therefore, they must remain in the same syllable. We call this syllable the **final *e* syllable**. For example, the final *e* syllable in the word *delete* is *lete*.

STEP 2

Transition to Longer Words

Help students transition from reading one-syllable to multisyllabic words. Have them read the simple word or syllable in the first column, then use that word or syllable to read the multi-syllabic word in the second column.

cade	arcade
ate	cooperate
vice	device
cline	decline
rode	erode
mane	humane
pete	compete
fide	confide
lite	impolite
clone	cyclone

STEP 3

Build Words

Write the following word parts on the board:

> *dis, re, grace, pute, like, place, vise, make*

Have student pairs combine the word parts to build as many words as possible. These and other words can be formed:

> *disgrace, dispute, repute, dislike, displace, replace, revise, remake*

STEP 4

Apply Decoding Strategy

Have students use the Decoding Big Words Strategy to decode the following words:

> *masquerade, impersonate, insecticide, valentine, saxophone*

Remind them to look for final *e* syllables in Step 3 of the strategy.

Name _____ Date _____

Final *e* Syllables What's My Word?

1. Read each clue.

2. Look at the incomplete word.

3. Write the missing letters to solve the clue.

(1) To finish   c ____ ____ p l ____ t ____

(2) To work together   c ____ o p e r ____ t ____

(3) To make again   r ____ m ____ k ____

(4) To not like   d ____ ____ l ____ k ____

(5) To make edits to your writing   r ____ v ____ s ____

(6) A lizard   r e ____ t ____ l ____

(7) To find   l o ____ ____ t ____

(8) To blow up a balloon   i n ____ l ____ t ____

(9) Will you be my _____ ?   v a l ____ ____ t ____ n ____

(10) A terrible wind and rain storm   c y ____ l ____ n ____

Name _____ Date _____

Final *e* Syllable Speed Drill

1. Underline the final *e* syllable in each word.
2. Pronounce each word with your teacher.
3. Practice reading the words on your own.
4. When you are ready, have a partner time you reading the words for one minute. Keep practicing to improve your speed.

supreme	stampede	textile	reptile	shameful	regulate	recite	sincerely	profile	lonesome
remote	locate	suppose	humane	inflate	secrete	extreme	estate	device	complete
reptile	regulate	stampede	complete	suppose	device	shameful	extreme	sincerely	textile
device	remote	sincerely	secrete	supreme	locate	inflate	humane	recite	estate
supreme	extreme	reptile	suppose	profile	inflate	stampede	locate	lonesome	shameful
regulate	secrete	remote	inflate	reptile	suppose	recite	lonesome	textile	humane
extreme	profile	regulate	sincerely	stampede	estate	lonesome	complete	locate	profile
humane	device	supreme	estate	recite	textile	profile	shameful	suppose	secrete
estate	recite	inflate	secrete	sincerely	lonesome	reptile	remote	supreme	complete
textile	extreme	shameful	regulate	complete	stampede	humane	device	remote	locate

	Words per Minute	Date	Partner
Timed Reading 1	_____	_____	_____
Timed Reading 2	_____	_____	_____
Timed Reading 3	_____	_____	_____

Name _____ Date _____

High-Frequency Syllable Fluency • Part 1

Read It

1. Underline the target syllable in each word.
2. Practice reading the words.
3. Cut apart the word cards.
4. See how fast you can sort the words by common syllable.

Syllables 251–260

wil	willow	Wilbur	wildebeest
win	window	winner	wintergreen
won	wonder	wonderful	wondrous
work	workplace	**framework**	**network**
act	overact	**react**	**interact**
ag	agriculture	agony	**aggregate**
air	airplane	airport	airtight
als	**visuals**	betrayals	**liberals**
bat	battle	battery	battleground
bi	bicycle	**bias**	bicentennial

● For Part 2, make a copy of the reproducible on page 159 for each student.

Suffixes Mini-lesson (-ity/-ty, -ment, -ic, -ous/-eous/-ious)

STEP 1

Define

Tell students that a **suffix** is a letter or group of letters added to the end of a base word. A suffix changes the word's meaning and often its part of speech. For example, the suffix *-ed* is added to the word *depart* (*departed*) to indicate that the action happened in the past. Point out the following suffixes:

- **-ity/-ty** used to mean "state of" (turns a root word into a noun)

    The employees showed great *loyalty* to their company.

- **-ment** used to indicate "action" or "process"

    We left the *development* of the house plans to the architect.

- **-ic** means "having characteristics of or having to do with" (historic), "like" (metallic), or "made of or with" (alcoholic)
    (turns a root word into an adjective)

    President Obama's election was *historic* for the United States

- **-ous/-eous/-ious** means "possessing the qualities of" or "full of"

    Driving in a snowstorm can be quite *dangerous*.

STEP 2

Transition to Longer Words

Help students transition from reading one-syllable to multisyllabic words. Have them read the suffix in the first column, then use that suffix to read the multisyllabic word in the second column.

ty	safety
ment	payment

ic	artistic
ous	marvelous
eous	nauseous
ity	humidity
ment	advertisement
ic	gymnastic
ious	curious
ious	cautious

STEP 3

Build Words

Write the following word parts on the board:

ty, ment, ic, ious, safe, loyal, uni, argu, move, settle, place, histor, rust, civ, graph, fur, infect, delic

Have student pairs combine the word parts to build as many words as possible. These and other words can be formed:

safety, loyalty, unity, argument, movement, settlement, placement, historic, rustic, civic, graphic, furious, infectious, delicious

STEP 4

Apply Decoding Strategy

Have students use the Decoding Big Words Strategy to decode the following words:

adventurous, subconscious, announcement, entertainment, mathematical

Remind them to look for suffixes in Step 2 of the strategy.

Name _____ Date _____

Suffixes Connect-a-Word (*-ity/-ty, -ment, -ic, -ous/-eous/-ious*)

1. Select one word part from each column to make a new word. Each word part can be used only once.
2. Write the new word in the last column.

Column 1	Column 2	Column 3	Word Formed
loy	mid	ic	
aca	lec	ment	
hu	ul	ity	
gov	al	ous	
e	i	tric	
fab	prove	ment	
ser	dem	ty	
im	ern	ous	

Name _____ Date _____

Suffix Speed Drill (-ity/-ty, -ment, -ic, -ous/-eous/-ious)

1. Underline the suffix that ends each word.
2. Pronounce each word with your teacher.
3. Practice reading the words on your own.
4. When you are ready, have a partner time you reading the words for one minute. Keep practicing to improve your speed.

honesty	humidity	agreement	academic	fabulous	nauseous	ambitious	loyalty	unity	equipment
obesity	safety	settlement	heroic	anonymous	gorgeous	furious	necessity	regularity	argument
academic	equipment	humidity	obesity	nauseous	fabulous	gorgeous	unity	honesty	loyalty
ambitious	agreement	anonymous	nauseous	heroic	obesity	settlement	fabulous	furious	safety
equipment	regularity	agreement	furious	unity	humidity	honesty	argument	loyalty	gorgeous
anonymous	ambitious	regularity	academic	settlement	heroic	obesity	gorgeous	humidity	necessity
unity	equipment	ambitious	honesty	regularity	loyalty	academic	nauseous	necessity	fabulous
necessity	loyalty	anonymous	ambitious	argument	agreement	heroic	obesity	safety	nauseous
settlement	honesty	equipment	fabulous	furious	necessity	safety	argument	academic	humidity
furious	settlement	unity	anonymous	safety	gorgeous	agreement	regularity	heroic	argument

	Words per Minute	Date	Partner
Timed Reading 1	_____	_____	_____
Timed Reading 2	_____	_____	_____
Timed Reading 3	_____	_____	_____

Name _____ Date _____

High-Frequency Syllable Fluency • Part 1

 Read It

1. Underline the target syllable in each word.
2. Practice reading the words.
3. Cut apart the word cards.
4. See how fast you can sort the words by common syllable.

Syllables 261–270

cate	dedicate	replicate	**communicate**
cen	center	century	**incentive**
char	charcoal	charter	charity*
come	become	**income**	unwelcome
cul	**culture**	cultivate	culprit
ders	ladders	wonders	elders
east	Easter	eastern	easterly
fect	affect	infect	disinfect
fish	fishbowl	fisherman	goldfishes
fix	fixing	fixture	fixation

● For Part 2, make a copy of the reproducible on page 159 for each student.

Review and Assess

Assessment Directions

1. Make one copy of the Real Word Test (page 134) and the Nonsense Word Test (page 135). You may wish to make the copy on cardstock for greater durability.

2. Make a copy of the Assessment Scoring Sheet (page 133) for each student.

3. Assess students individually. Have each student read the words from the Real Word Test, then the Nonsense Word Test.

4. Place a checkmark (✓) in the second column for each word read correctly. If the student correctly reads the word but does so in a slow, labored manner, place a check minus (✓–) in the second column to indicate that fluency (automaticity with the sound-spellings) may still be an issue.

5. If the student incorrectly reads the word, record the attempt. Analyze the errors to notice patterns of difficulty. For example, some students might be overrelying on the initial letters in a word and not fully analyzing it. Other students might have difficulties with one specific aspect of the word, such as a complex spelling pattern. This analysis will inform the next steps you take to address these issues. During small-group instructional time, continue working with students on those skills not mastered.

6. Tally the scores from both tests. Students should be able to read the words with a minimum of 80% accuracy (i.e., 24 correct out of 30).

7. Create an Action Plan for students who struggle with specific skills (accuracy or speed issues) or students who fall below the 80% level. These students will need additional instruction, practice, and review on the skills covered in the lessons.

Assessment Scoring Sheet

Place a checkmark (✓) in the second column if the student reads the word correctly. If the student correctly reads the word but does so in a slow, labored manner, place a check minus (✓–) in the second column. If the student reads the word incorrectly, record the student's attempt.

Student Name: _____

Date: _____

Real Word Test	
1. marble	
2. vertical	
3. collide	
4. translate	
5. decode	
6. prejudge	
7. invisible	
8. valuable	
9. accidental	
10. octagon	
11. uniform	
12. urgently	
13. vaporize	
14. regulate	
15. complete	
16. argument	
17. advertisement	
18. fabulous	
19. honesty	
20. gymnastics	

Nonsense Word Test	
1. churbit	
2. napsate	
3. parthlet	
4. wolide	
5. verzeck	
6. slibment	
7. grizzable	
8. lemness	
9. blagulous	
10. interslesh	

Scores: _____ Real Word Test

_____ Nonsense Word Test

_____ Total Score

Fluency: ❏ Good

❏ Poor

Skills Needing Additional Work:

Action Plan:

Name _____ Date _____

Real Word Test

1. marble	11. uniform
2. vertical	12. urgently
3. collide	13. vaporize
4. translate	14. regulate
5. decode	15. complete
6. prejudge	16. argument
7. invisible	17. advertisement
8. valuable	18. fabulous
9. accidental	19. honesty
10. octagon	20. gymnastics

Name _____ Date _____

Nonsense Word Test

1. churbit

2. napsate

3. parthlet

4. wolide

5. verzeck

6. slibment

7. grizzable

8. lemness

9. blagulous

10. interslesh

Prefixes Mini-lesson (*trans-, super-, semi-*)

 STEP 1

Define

Tell students that a **prefix** is a group of letters added to the beginning of a base word to make a new word. The prefix changes the word's meaning. Recognizing common prefixes can help students decode a word and figure out its meaning. For example, the word *unhappy* begins with the prefix *un-*. The prefix *un-* means "not" or "the opposite of." So, someone who is unhappy is <u>not</u> happy. Point out the following prefixes:

- **trans-** means "across"
  The *transcontinental* railroad ran across the entire United States.
- **super-** means "above"
  The comic hero had *superhuman* powers.
- **semi-** means "half"
  The horse escaped because the barn door was only *semiclosed*.

 STEP 2

Transition to Longer Words

Help students transition from reading one-syllable to multisyllabic words. Have them read the prefix in the first column, then use that prefix to read and define the multisyllabic word in the second column.

trans	transplant
super	superfast
semi	semidry
trans	transmit
super	supersize
semi	semifinal

 STEP 3

Build Words

Write the following word parts on the board:

> *trans, super, semi, fer, mit, plant,*
> *clean, heat, fast, power, dry, closed,*
> *weekly, final*

Have student pairs combine the word parts to build as many words as possible. These and other words can be formed:

> *transfer, transmit, transplant,*
> *superclean, superheat, superfast,*
> *semidry, semiclosed, semiweekly,*
> *semifinal*

 STEP 4

Apply Decoding Strategy

Have students use the Decoding Big Words Strategy to decode the following words:

> *transatlantic, superabsorbent, supersensitive,*
> *semiautomatic, semidangerous*

Remind them to look for prefixes in Step 1 of the strategy.

Name _____ Date _____

Prefixes Crossword Puzzle *(trans-, super-, semi-)*

1. Read the puzzle clues.
2. To answer each clue, select from the words in the box.
3. Write the correct word in the puzzle.

semiclosed
semidry
semifinal
superfast
superhuman
supersafe
transatlantic
transmit
transplant
transport

Across

3. to move an organ, such as a heart, from one body to another
6. about halfway dry
7. very safe
8. across the Atlantic Ocean
9. unbelievably quick

Down

1. to carry goods across borders
2. to carry messages from one place to another
4. abilities greater than the average person
5. halfway to the finals of a sports event
6. half shut

Name _____ Date _____

Prefix Speed Drill *(trans-, super-, semi-)*

1. Underline the prefix that begins each word.
2. Pronounce each word with your teacher.
3. Practice reading the words on your own.
4. When you are ready, have a partner time you reading the words for one minute. Keep practicing to improve your speed.

transfer	supersize	semisweet	transatlantic	superfast	semifinal	transmit	superhuman	semipro	transplant
supernatural	semiautomatic	transition	supersensitive	semicircle	transcontinental	superman	semidry	transport	supersonic
transition	transcontinental	transfer	transport	supersensitive	semidry	semisweet	supersonic	superfast	superhuman
supersize	supersonic	supernatural	semicircle	transfer	semipro	supersensitive	transatlantic	superman	transmit
semiautomatic	semicircle	semipro	semidry	supernatural	superfast	superhuman	supersensitive	semisweet	transport
semifinal	semidry	supersize	transition	superhuman	semiautomatic	transfer	transmit	transplant	superman
semicircle	semipro	semifinal	superfast	supersize	supernatural	transplant	semiautomatic	supersensitive	transatlantic
superhuman	supersonic	semisweet	transcontinental	semifinal	superman	transmit	transition	transfer	transport
semipro	semisweet	superman	transmit	transplant	transatlantic	transport	supernatural	transcontinental	transition
transcontinental	superfast	transplant	transatlantic	semidry	semicircle	supersize	semifinal	supersonic	semiautomatic

	Words per Minute	Date	Partner
Timed Reading 1	_____	_____	_____
Timed Reading 2	_____	_____	_____
Timed Reading 3	_____	_____	_____

Name _____ Date _____

High-Frequency Syllable Fluency • Part 1

 Read It

1. Underline the target syllable in each word.
2. Practice reading the words.
3. Cut apart the word cards.
4. See how fast you can sort the words by common syllable.

Syllables 271–280

gi	giant	gigantic	fungi*
grand	grandfather	grandstand	grand jury
great	greatest	greatness	great-grandchild
heav	heavy	heaven	heavenly
ho	hotel	holy	hogan
hunt	hunter	overhunted	headhunter
ion	onion	million	union
its	edits	credits	exhibits
jo	banjo	Joseph	jovial
lat	latter	Latin	latitude

● For Part 2, make a copy of the reproducible on page 159 for each student.

Suffixes Mini-lesson (-en, -er, -ive/-ative/-itive)

STEP 1

Define

Tell students that a **suffix** is a letter or group of letters added to the end of a base word. A suffix changes the word's meaning and often its part of speech. For example, the suffix -ed is added to the word depart (departed) to indicate that the action happened in the past. Point out the following suffixes:

- **-en** means "made of" (often spelling changes are required when adding this suffix)

  The meat was too *frozen* to cook right away.

- **-er** is used to compare two things; "more" (often spelling changes are required when adding this suffix)

  The building is *bigger* than our school.

- **-ive/-ative/-itive** means "tending to do something" (makes the adjective form of a noun)

  The dog was so *active*, it wore us out.

STEP 2

Transition to Longer Words

Help students transition from reading one-syllable to multisyllabic words. Have them read the suffix in the first column, then use that suffix to read the multisyllabic word in the second column.

en	soften	er	brighter
ive	active	ative	talkative

 Teacher-to-Teacher

itive	additive	en	bitten
er	funnier	ive	secretive
ative	narrative	itive	repetitive

STEP 3

Build Words

Write the following suffixes on the board in random order:

en, er, ive, ative, itive

Have student pairs add these suffixes to the following words to build as many words as possible:

happy, sad, quick, broke, hid, sharp, digest, define, instruct, talk

Have them check a dictionary for spelling. These and other words can be formed:

happier, sadder, quicker, broken, hidden, sharpen, digestive, definitive, instructive, talkative

STEP 4

Apply Decoding Strategy

Have students use the Decoding Big Words Strategy to decode the following words:

narrower, straightening, hyperactive, locomotive, representative

Remind them to look for suffixes in Step 2 of the strategy.

Spelling Changes: Focus on spelling changes when adding these suffixes to base words.

Name _____ Date _____

Suffixes Unscramble It! (*-en, -er, -ive/-ative/-itive*)

1. Unscramble each set of letters to form a word with a suffix.

2. Write the words in the blank.

(1) er   hap   pi   _____

(2) ti   er   pret   _____

(3) hid   un   den   _____

(4) sharp   en   re   _____

(5) pet   com   itive   _____

(6) act   re   ive   _____

(7) ef   ive   fect   _____

(8) tive   nar   ra   _____

(9) ive   gest   di   _____

(10) cript   des   ive   _____

Name _____ Date _____

Suffix Speed Drill (-en, -er, -ive/-ative/-itive)

1. Underline the suffix that ends each word.
2. Pronounce each word with your teacher.
3. Practice reading the words on your own.
4. When you are ready, have a partner time you reading the words for one minute.
   Keep practicing to improve your speed.

broken	higher	captive	talkative	repetitive	straighten	narrower	disruptive	native	fugitive
barren	straighter	descriptive	tentative	sensitive	enlighten	prettier	inactive	motive	executive
executive	inactive	straighter	broken	tentative	descriptive	talkative	sensitive	narrower	disruptive
captive	barren	straighten	straighter	enlighten	higher	native	repetitive	fugitive	sensitive
enlighten	motive	barren	captive	disruptive	broken	narrower	prettier	descriptive	repetitive
tentative	talkative	executive	native	straighten	fugitive	straighter	higher	executive	descriptive
inactive	tentative	narrower	disruptive	captive	barren	straighten	broken	prettier	straighter
motive	disruptive	native	repetitive	motive	talkative	sensitive	inactive	higher	prettier
narrower	repetitive	enlighten	tentative	fugitive	prettier	captive	barren	straighten	higher
executive	fugitive	inactive	native	sensitive	descriptive	enlighten	talkative	motive	broken

	Words per Minute	Date	Partner
Timed Reading 1	_____	_____	_____
Timed Reading 2	_____	_____	_____
Timed Reading 3	_____	_____	_____

Name _____ Date _____

High-Frequency Syllable Fluency • Part 1

Read It

1. Underline the target syllable in each word.
2. Practice reading the words.
3. Cut apart the word cards.
4. See how fast you can sort the words by common syllable.

Syllables 281–290

lead	leader	leadership	misleading
lect	elect	**select**	collectible
lent	excellent	relentless	**equivalent**
less	restless	hopeless	carelessness
lin	linen	gremlin	linear
mal	**normal**	**minimal**	malnutrition
mi	minus	**minor**	**migrate**
mil	million	**military**	mildew
moth	mother*	mammoth	behemoth
near	nearest	nearby	nearsighted

● For Part 2, make a copy of the reproducible on page 159 for each student.

Greek and Latin Roots Mini-lesson (body parts)

STEP 1

Define

Tell students that a **root** is a basic word part that gives a word the most important part of its meaning. Many English words have roots from Greek, the language of the people from ancient Greece. For example, the Greek roots *auto* and *graph* are used to form the word *autograph*.

Many English words also have roots from Latin, the language of the ancient Romans. For example, the Latin root *port* is used to form the word *portable*. Teach the meanings of the following Greek and Latin roots:

- **caput** means "head" (capital, decapitate)
- **gurges** means "throat" (gurgle, regurgitate)
- **os, oris** mean "mouth" (oral, orifice, oratory)
- **dens, dentis** mean "teeth" (dental, dentist)
- **carnis** means "flesh" (carnal, carnage)
- **corpus** means "body" (corporal punishment, corpse)
- **cordis** means "heart" (courage, encourage, cordial)
- **derma** means "skin" (dermatology, epidermis)
- **gaster** means "stomach" (gastric)
- **manus** means "hand" (manipulate, command, demand, manage, manual, maneuver)
- **digitus** means "finger" (digit, digital)
- **pes, pedis** mean "foot" (pedal, moped, pedestrian, pedicure)

STEP 2

Transition to Longer Words

Help students transition from reading one-syllable to multisyllabic words. Have them read the root in the first column, then use that root to read and define the multisyllabic word in the second column. Model as needed.

caput	capital
dentis	dentist
cordis	cordial
gaster	gastric
digitus	digital
oris	oral
corpus	corpse
derma	dermatology
manus	manage
pedis	pedicure

STEP 3

Build Words

Write the following word parts on the board in random order:

> *man, ped, date, ipulate, age, ner, icure, ual, al, mo, igree*

Have student pairs use the word parts to build as many words as possible. These and other words can be formed:

> *mandate, manipulate, manage, manner, manual, manicure, pedicure, pedal, moped, pedigree*

STEP 4

Apply Decoding Strategy

Have students use the Decoding Big Words Strategy to decode the following words:

> *pedestrian, dermatologist, capitalize, dentistry, manufactured*

Remind them to look for Greek and Latin roots in Step 3 of the strategy.

Name _____ Date _____

Greek and Latin Roots Greek and Latin Dictionary
(body parts)

1. Using what you know about Greek and Latin roots, write a definition for each word.
2. Work with a partner.
3. Look up the word in a dictionary.
4. Record the dictionary definition under your definition.

Word: dermatologist

My Definition: _____

Dictionary Definition: _____

_____

Word: manufacture

My Definition: _____

Dictionary Definition: _____

_____

Word: pedestrian

My Definition: _____

Dictionary Definition: _____

_____

Word: corporal punishment

My Definition: _____

Dictionary Definition: _____

_____

Word: cordial

My Definition: _____

Dictionary Definition: _____

_____

Name _____ Date _____

Greek and Latin Root Speed Drill (body parts)

1. Underline the Greek and Latin body part root in each word.
2. Pronounce each word with your teacher.
3. Practice reading the words on your own.
4. When you are ready, have a partner time you reading the words for one minute. Keep practicing to improve your speed.

dental	octopus	dermatology	courage	podium	corpse	podiatrist	capital	manual	gurgle
oral	orthodontist	carnivorous	corporal	gastric	manicure	digit	pedal	pedestrian	orifice
carnivorous	dental	podiatrist	manicure	octopus	gastric	corpse	digit	capital	podium
manicure	manual	oral	orthodontist	courage	corpse	gastric	podium	corporal	pedal
dermatology	podiatrist	manicure	dental	corporal	oral	octopus	gastric	dermatology	gurgle
corpse	carnivorous	courage	digit	orthodontist	podium	pedestrian	gurgle	gastric	capital
manual	dermatology	carnivorous	manicure	dental	capital	oral	octopus	orifice	dermatology
podiatrist	digit	manual	podium	gurgle	orifice	corporal	orthodontist	oral	pedal
digit	corpse	pedestrian	courage	capital	dental	orifice	pedal	octopus	pedestrian
courage	orifice	podiatrist	gurgle	carnivorous	manual	pedal	pedestrian	orthodontist	corporal

	Words per Minute	Date	Partner
Timed Reading 1	_____	_____	_____
Timed Reading 2	_____	_____	_____
Timed Reading 3	_____	_____	_____

Name _____ Date _____

High-Frequency Syllable Fluency • Part 1

 Read It

1. Underline the target syllable in each word.
2. Practice reading the words.
3. Cut apart the word cards.
4. See how fast you can sort the words by common syllable.

Syllables 291–300

nel	funnel	**channel**	kernel
net	networks	magnet	cabinet
new	newly	newbie	newborn
one	someone	one-way	anyone
point	pointed	appoint	pointless
prac	practice	practical	impractical
ral	rally*	spiral	referral
rect	direct	erect	indirect
ried	carried	married	salaried
round	around	roundabout	roundup

● For Part 2, make a copy of the reproducible on page 159 for each student.

Prefixes Mini-lesson (*anti-, mid-, under-*)

STEP 1

Define

Tell students that a **prefix** is a group of letters added to the beginning of a base word to make a new word. The prefix changes the word's meaning. Recognizing common prefixes can help students decode a word and figure out its meaning. For example, the word *unhappy* begins with the prefix *un-*. The prefix *un-* means "not" or "the opposite of." So, someone who is unhappy is <u>not</u> happy. Point out the following prefixes:

- **anti-** means "against" (antiwar), or "working against" (antiperspirant) (When the word begins with a capital letter, a hyphen is used, as in anti-American.)

  The doctor looked for the *antidote* to the poison.

- **mid-** means "middle"

  We stopped *midway* on our trip to eat lunch.

- **under-** means "too little" or "beneath"

  The skinny dog looked as if it had been *underfed*.

STEP 2

Transition to Longer Words

Help students transition from reading one-syllable to multisyllabic words. Have them read the prefix in the first column, then use that prefix to read and define the multisyllabic word in the second column. Model as needed.

anti	anticrime
mid	midsize
under	underage

anti	antiwar
mid	midyear
under	underdog

STEP 3

Build Words

Write the following word parts on the board:

anti, mid, under, crime, war, dote, day, life, week, term, age, cook, cover, shirt, way

Have student pairs use the word parts to build as many words as possible. These and other words can be formed:

anticrime, antiwar, antidote, midday, midlife, midweek, midterm, underage, undercook, undercover, undershirt, underway

STEP 4

Apply Decoding Strategy

Have students use the Decoding Big Words Strategy to decode the following words:

antiperspirant, midafternoon, underachieve, underestimate, underdeveloped

Remind them to look for prefixes in Step 1 of the strategy.

Name _____ Date _____

Prefixes B-I-N-G-O (anti-, mid-, under-)

1. Write one of the following words randomly in each blank on the B-I-N-G-O board:

> *antibacterial, antidote, antiperspirant, antisocial, midcourse, midnight, midsized, midweek, undercover, underdog, underground, underpay*

You may use a word more than once.

2. Mark each word on the board as your teacher calls it.

B	I	N	G	O
		FREE		

Name _____ Date _____

Prefix Speed Drill *(anti-, mid-, under-)*

1. Underline the prefix that begins each word.
2. Pronounce each word with your teacher.
3. Practice reading the words on your own.
4. When you are ready, have a partner time you reading the words for one minute. Keep practicing to improve your speed.

anticrime	midday	underage	antisocial	midafternoon	underbrush	antigravity	midcourse	undercharge	antiwar
midnight	undercook	antibacterial	midsize	underclothes	midweek	underpay	midyear	understudy	underground
antisocial	midsize	anticrime	underclothes	antibacterial	underage	underbrush	undercharge	antigravity	midcourse
midday	midnight	midafternoon	undercook	antigravity	midsize	antibacterial	underage	underbrush	underpay
antigravity	midyear	midnight	understudy	anticrime	undercharge	undercook	underpay	midcourse	underclothes
midyear	antisocial	midday	undercharge	underground	midafternoon	underpay	midcourse	antiwar	underage
midweek	antigravity	midyear	midcourse	midnight	understudy	anticrime	antiwar	undercook	underground
underpay	midweek	antisocial	antibacterial	midday	antiwar	underground	midafternoon	understudy	undercook
antibacterial	underage	midweek	underclothes	antiwar	midsize	midnight	midyear	anticrime	underbrush
underclothes	underground	undercharge	midweek	antisocial	understudy	midsize	midday	underbrush	midafternoon

	Words per Minute	Date	Partner
Timed Reading 1	_____	_____	_____
Timed Reading 2	_____	_____	_____
Timed Reading 3	_____	_____	_____

Name _____ Date _____

High-Frequency Syllable Fluency • Part 1

 Read It

1. Underline the target syllable in each word.
2. Practice reading the words.
3. Cut apart the word cards.
4. See how fast you can sort the words by common syllable.

Syllables 301–310

row	rowboat	arrow	rowdy*
sa	sensation	sabertooth tiger	saliva*
sand	sandy	sandstorm	sandwiches
self	myself	selfish	self-defense
sent	absent	resentful*	consent
ship	shipment	friendship	scholarship
sim	simple	similar	simulate
sions	visions	decisions	commissions
sis	sister	thesis	hypothesis
sons	persons	poisons	bisons

● For Part 2, make a copy of the reproducible on page 159 for each student.

Suffixes Mini-lesson (-ful, -less, -est)

Define

Tell students that a **suffix** is a letter or group of letters added to the end of a base word. A suffix changes the word's meaning and often its part of speech. For example, the suffix -ed is added to the word *depart* (*departed*) to indicate that the action happened in the past. Point out the following suffixes:

- **-ful** used to indicate "full of" (careful), "able to" (harmful), "as much as will fill" (cupful)
  We were *careful* not to break the glasses.
  That chemical is *harmful* to pets.

- **-less** used to indicate "without" (doubtless, effortless) or "unable to be" (countless)
  Winning the game seemed *effortless* for our great soccer team.

- **-est** used as a comparative (three or more items); "most"
  That is the *biggest* dog I have ever seen.

Transition to Longer Words

Help students transition from reading one-syllable to multisyllabic words. Have them read the suffix in the first column, then use that suffix to read the multisyllabic word in the second column.

ful	wonderful
less	priceless
est	warmest
ful	colorful
less	scoreless
est	widest

Build Words

Write the following word parts on the board:

> *ful, less, est, age, bone, color, life, arm, care, joy, skill, clean, cold, smooth, straight*

Have student pairs use the word parts to build as many words as possible. These and other words can be formed:

> *ageless, boneless, colorful, colorless, lifeless, armful, careful, careless, joyful, skillful, cleanest, coldest, smoothest, straightest*

Apply Decoding Strategy

Have students use the Decoding Big Words Strategy to decode the following words:

> *healthiest, unsuccessful, beautiful, hopelessness, thoughtlessly*

Remind them to look for suffixes in Step 2 of the strategy.

Name _____ Date _____

Suffixes Build-a-Word (-*ful, -less, -est*)

1. Add one of the following suffixes to the base word to form new words: -*ful, -less, -est*.
2. Remember that spelling changes might be necessary.
3. Check the spelling using a dictionary.

Base Word	New Word(s) Formed
color	
wide	
beauty	
thought	
wonder	
straight	
care	
use	
hope	
doubt	

Name _____ Date _____

Suffix Speed Drill (-ful, -less, -est)

1. Underline the suffix that ends each word.
2. Pronounce each word with your teacher.
3. Practice reading the words on your own.
4. When you are ready, have a partner time you reading the words for one minute. Keep practicing to improve your speed.

armful	careless	brightest	beautiful	endless	earliest	doubtful	hopeless	busiest	healthful
painless	happiest	graceful	weightless	freshest	peaceful	mindless	softest	colorful	worthless
beautiful	busiest	armful	graceful	doubtful	endless	freshest	healthful	earliest	mindless
brightest	painless	busiest	happiest	careless	weightless	graceful	earliest	mindless	hopeless
peaceful	softest	brightest	colorful	painless	armful	healthful	endless	careless	freshest
doubtful	beautiful	peaceful	busiest	healthful	hopeless	worthless	happiest	endless	weightless
softest	worthless	beautiful	hopeless	brightest	colorful	earliest	mindless	armful	graceful
hopeless	doubtful	softest	healthful	busiest	painless	brightest	weightless	happiest	colorful
colorful	mindless	armful	peaceful	doubtful	freshest	graceful	painless	worthless	careless
earliest	worthless	weightless	beautiful	careless	peaceful	happiest	softest	freshest	endless

	Words per Minute	Date	Partner
Timed Reading 1	_____	_____	_____
Timed Reading 2	_____	_____	_____
Timed Reading 3	_____	_____	_____

Name _____ Date _____

High-Frequency Syllable Fluency • Part 1

Read It

1. Underline the target syllable in each word.
2. Practice reading the words.
3. Cut apart the word cards.
4. See how fast you can sort the words by common syllable.

Syllables 311–322

stand	standard	withstand	notwithstanding
sug	suggest	suggestion	suggestive
tel	telephone	television	intelligent
tom	bottom	atomic	tomboyish
tors	actors	tractors	curators
tract	distract	contract	extract
tray	ashtray	portray	betraying
us	status	sinus	ruckus
vel	velvet	Velcro	development
west	westward	midwestern	westernize
where	nowhere	whereas	whereabouts
writ	written	unwritten	rewritten

● For Part 2, make a copy of the reproducible on page 159 for each student.

Review and Assess

Assessment Directions

1. Make one copy of the Real Word Test (page 158) and the Nonsense Word Test (page 158). You may wish to make the copy on cardstock for greater durability.

2. Make one copy of the Assessment Scoring Sheet (page 157) for each student.

3. Assess students individually. Have each student read the words from the Real Word Test, then the Nonsense Word Test.

4. Place a checkmark (✓) in the second column for each word read correctly. If the student correctly reads the word but does so in a slow, labored manner, place a check minus (✓–) in the second column to indicate that fluency (automaticity with the sound-spellings) may still be an issue.

5. If the student incorrectly reads the word, record the attempt. Analyze the errors to notice patterns of difficulty. For example, some students might be overrelying on the initial letters in a word and not fully analyzing it. Other students might have difficulties with one specific aspect of the word, such as a complex spelling pattern. This analysis will inform the next steps you take to address these issues. During small-group instructional time, continue working with students on those skills not mastered.

6. Tally the scores from both tests. Students should be able to read the words with a minimum of 80% accuracy (i.e., 12 out of 15 correct).

7. Create an Action Plan for students who struggle with specific skills (accuracy or speed issues) or students who fall below the 80% level. These students will need additional instruction, practice, and review on the skills covered in the lessons.

Assessment Scoring Sheet

Place a checkmark (✓) in the second column if the student reads the word correctly. If the student correctly reads the word but does so in a slow, labored manner, place a check minus (✓–) in the second column. If the student reads the word incorrectly, record the student's attempt.

Student Name: _____

Date: _____

Real Word Test	
1. transplant	
2. semifinal	
3. brighter	
4. softening	
5. talkative	
6. secretive	
7. manufacture	
8. anticrime	
9. underage	
10. hopelessness	

Nonsense Word Test	
1. superglex	
2. duflessly	
3. geckative	
4. manupex	
5. antilepshum	

Scores: _____ Real Word Test

_____ Nonsense Word Test

_____ Total Score

Fluency: ❑ Good

❑ Poor

Skills Needing Additional Work:

Action Plan:

Name _____ Date _____

Real Word Test

1. transplant

2. semifinal

3. brighter

4. softening

5. talkative

6. secretive

7. manufacture

8. anticrime

9. underage

10. hopelessness

Nonsense Word Test

1. superglex

2. duflessly

3. geckative

4. manupex

5. antilepshum

Name _____ Date _____

High-Frequency Syllable Fluency • Part 2

 Find It

1. Look in books and stories for words with this week's syllables.
2. Write the words you find below and underline the target syllable.

_____ _____ _____ _____

_____ _____ _____ _____

_____ _____ _____ _____

 Define It

1. Look at this week's word cards. Choose five words that you don't know the meanings of or that you would like to know more about.
2. Fill in the table with each word, its definition, a synonym, and a sample sentence.

Word	Meaning	Synonym	Sentence
Example: order	to ask for	command, request	On Sundays, I order scrambled eggs for breakfast at the diner.

Answer Key

page 21: 1. pencil, 2. absent, 3. plastic, 4. rabbit, 5. witness, 6. cactus, 7. dentist, 8. exit, 9. mittens, 10. suffix

page 25: Across: 3. lethal, 5. locate, 7. donate, 8. grocery, 9. frequent; Down: 1. solo, 2. zebra, 4. hibernate, 5. lazy, 6. prefix

page 29: Students should place an X over the following words: 1. uncle, 2. realize, 3. indicate, 4. important, 5. iron, 6. illustrate, 7. under, 8. restful, 9. inches, 10. impala, 11. Iroquois, 12. illusion; sentences will vary but should include a prefixed word.

page 33: plants, planted, planting; stops, stopped, stopping; blames, blamed, blaming; stays, stayed, staying; rhymes, rhymed, rhyming; watches, watched, watching; brushes, brushed, brushing; dresses, dressed, dressing; touches, touched, touching; quizzes, quizzed, quizzing

page 37: Students should write the words in random order on the BINGO board.

page 41: Students should write the dictionary definition for each word. Their self-generated definitions should include the concept of "carrying" material, people, or information from one place to another.

page 45: 1. fantastic, 2. improvement, 3. habitat, 4. independent, 5. watermelon, 6. commonly, 7. contestant, 8. gossiping, 9. unhidden, 10. problematic

page 49:

i	l	f	u	t	u	r	e	p	v
m	e	r	e	n	a	g	o	l	s
l	v	h	r	p	h	f	v	i	o
a	h	u	g	i	e	f	t	p	c
t	s	m	t	h	l	u	h	l	i
i	f	a	v	o	r	i	t	e	a
v	i	n	c	r	s	l	o	g	l
u	f	a	e	o	i	l	a	a	w
t	t	r	l	a	h	t	e	l	u
e	s	o	f	u	x	v	i	x	h
l	o	e	l	a	m	e	f	b	o
l	f	u	v	m	k	e	p	v	t
o	o	s	a	t	s	l	o	z	o
r	e	c	e	n	t	l	y	e	h
r	t	n	t	s	o	v	t	l	p

page 57: 1. apple, 2. giggle, 3. fable, 4. eagle, 5. middle, 6. simple, 7. uncle, 8. wiggle, 9. beetle, 10. cattle; 11.–12. Clues will vary, but solutions should end with consonant + -le.

page 61: Across: 2. monkey, 4. employee, 6. barefoot, 7. unafraid, 8. oatmeal, 9. monsoon; Down: 1. playground, 2. mistreat, 3. exclaim, 5. poison

page 65: The following words can be formed: disappear, dishonest, disagree, employed, enjoying, encourage, nonfiction, nontoxic.

page 69: Possible Words: dreamily, dreamer, collector, collection, creation, creator, sleeper, sleepily, directly, direction, illustration, illustrator, exhibitor, exhibition, demonstrator, demonstration, subscription, subscriber, collision, collider

page 73: Students should write the words in random order on the BINGO board.

page 77: Students should write the dictionary definition for each word. Their self-generated definitions should include the meaning of the Latin root.

page 81:

n	b	r	i	t	z	p	r	i	t
o	g	e	l	b	m	e	s	s	a
o	b	o	t	l	b	d	p	e	m
p	r	n	o	o	u	b	l	e	d
r	i	z	z	r	n	t	i	l	p
p	t	b	a	l	d	e	n	o	u
l	t	b	l	e	l	v	o	c	r
e	l	o	e	e	n	t	c	p
e	e	t	z	u	p	r	i	i	l
l	w	t	p	z	z	l	t	h	e
c	z	l	n	o	o	d	l	e	t
i	s	e	m	b	l	e	e	v	n
h	s	s	o	t	t	l	b	d	r
e	l	z	z	u	p	u	r	p	p
v	u	n	d	e	l	z	z	v	u

page 85: 1. yesterday, 2. battleground, 3. appointment, 4. holiday, 5. entertain, 6. complaining, 7. maintaining, 8. magnified, 9. proofreading, 10. needlepoint

page 89: 1. overcook, 2. misread, 3. subway, 4. indoors, 5. misplaced, 6. submarine, 7. mistreat, 8. import, 9. overheat, 10. immigrant

page 97: 1. artist, 2. barber, 3. circus, 4. garden, 5. doctor, 6. dinner, 7. enter, 8. monster, 9. urban, 10. forty

page 101:

p	i	f	e	q	d	m	n	x	i
c	n	e	h	w	f	k	l	f	n
o	s	l	e	n	i	l	e	f	w
m	c	o	m	v	t	m	g	h	e
b	f	f	e	h	a	h	y	r	a
i	e	t	e	l	h	t	a	i	s
n	t	r	e	m	n	l	n	n	e
e	r	a	a	e	v	e	f	l	i
e	e	i	a	s	w	g	e	e	n
a	d	v	i	c	e	f	r	r	s
d	a	s	b	n	m	d	e	e	i
s	v	m	o	c	e	v	v	f	d
i	n	c	o	m	p	l	e	t	e
x	i	y	u	i	o	p	s	d	s
w	g	j	c	o	a	t	h	l	d

page 105: Students should place an X over the following words: 1. presents, 2. interesting, 3. decorate, 4. interior, 5. precious, 6. deposit, 7. forensic, 8. decisions, 9. presentation, 10. foreign, 11. internal, 12. forest

page 109: Students should write the words in random order on the BINGO board.

page 113: Possible words include triangle, trilogy, trisect, trisection, trisector, triumvirate, tricycle, trillion, trimester, triple, triplet, triplicate, tricentennial, trident, triennial, trinity, tripartite, triplex, triptych.

page 117: 1. Possible words include unanimous, unanimity, unanimously, unilateral, unilaterally, unicorn, unicycle, uniform, unify, unique, unit, universal, union, unite, universe, university, unisex, unison, unitary.

page 121: Across: 3. vapor, 5. remark, 6. garlic, 10. turkey, Down: 1. razor, 2. nocturnal, 4. urgent, 7. arson, 8. urban, 9. hermit

page 125: 1. complete, 2. cooperate, 3. remake, 4. dislike, 5. revise, 6. reptile, 7. locate, 8. inflate, 9. valentine, 10. cyclone

page 129: The following words can be formed: loyalty, academic, humidity, government, electric, fabulous, serious, improvement.

page 137: Across: 3. transplant, 6. semidry, 7. supersafe, 8. transatlantic, 9. superfast, Down: 1. transport, 2. transmit, 4. superhuman, 5. semifinal, 6. semiclosed

page 141: 1. happier, 2. prettier, 3. unhidden, 4. resharpen, 5. competitive, 6. reactive, 7. effective, 8. narrative, 9. digestive, 10. descriptive

page 145: 1. Students should write the dictionary definition for each word. Their self-generated definitions should include the meaning of the Greek or Latin root.

page 149: Students write the words in random order on the BINGO board in order to play the game with the class

page 153: The following words can be formed: colorful, colorless, widest, beautiful, thoughtless, thoughtful, wonderful, straightest, careful, careless, useful, useless, hopeful, hopeless, doubtful, doubtless